LOUDOUN DISCOVERED

Communities, Corners
&
Crossroads

LOUDOUN DISCOVERED

Volume One
Eastern Loudoun: 'Goin' Down the Country'

Eugene M. Scheel

Presented by
The Friends of the Thomas Balch Library
Leesburg, Virginia

This book was manufactured in the United States of America.
Library of Congress Cataloging-in-Publication Data

Scheel, Eugene
        Loudoun discovered: communities, corners, and crossroads /
        vol. 1 eastern Loudoun "goin' down the country"
        Bibliography: p.
        Includes index.
        ISBN 0-0724754-0-0 (pbk.)

Cover design by Suzanne Stanton Chadwick
Chadwick Design Incorporated

Cover art from a mural painting by William Woodward

Book design by Janet MacDonald Manthos

Contents

List of Maps

Foreword

The Revolutionary War, the Civil War, the Civil Rights Movement, and many of our nation's other major events have directly impacted Loudoun County. Its history, however, has been shaped largely by the individuals and groups of people who settled and developed the county. *Loudoun Discovered* is a collection of the stories of this early settlement and development and of the gradual transition of crossroads and communities into villages and towns.

In 1975, Eugene Scheel, asked Jim Birchfield, editor of the *Loudoun Times-Mirror* if he could write a series of articles on the history of every town, village, and crossroads hamlet in Loudoun. They would be published to coincide with the U. S. Bicentennial. From his large collection of oral histories and extensive research into court records, church documents, and old maps, Gene developed very rich material, and he produced some 120 articles.

Gene's articles explained why particular settlements began and how they grew or languished. The stories brought out, among other things, how the establishment of trunpike roads and post offices affected development hundreds of years ago. In the 19th-century railroads played this role. During the past 50-or-so-years, it has been modern highways, waater and sewer lines, and airports.

The first broad documentation of the contribution of African Americans to the heritage of Loudoun County was presented in Gene's articles. His stories of the very small African American communities, such as St. Louis, Conklin, and Stewartown, brought them new and deserved recognition.

Late last year, Marty Hiatt, a respected genealogist and a good friend of the Thomas Balch Library, suggested to me that the Friends of the Library publish Gene's articles in book form. For more than 10 years, Marty had wanted to do this on her own. Her thought had been to use the book to raise funds for the Library. Marty had, in fact, taken the first steps on the project: she had scanned all of the articles and converted them into electronic form for editing.

I found strong support for taking on this project from fellow members of the Friends' Board. In addition, the Board members came up with some excellent suggestions for the books—adding maps and a comprehensive index, for example. And the stories would be organized by regions of the county so they could be published in five volumes that were relatively inexpensive and thus appealing to a broad audience.

The team assembled to prepare the articles for publication consisted of Gene Scheel, Marty Hiatt, Margaret Clarridge and Janet Manthos. Gene's assignment was to update and edit all of the articles and prepare the maps, some 25 among the five volumes. Marty provided guidance and counsel. Margaret checked spelling, punctuation, and consistancy, and Janet handled the desktop publishing, located photographs, prepared the index, and dealt with the printer. The Friends very much appreciate the efforts of these four individuals. They have certainly worked as a team.

The Friends give a special thank you to Arthur Arundel, publisher of the *Loudoun Times-Mirror,* for approving the request to publish Gene Scheel's articles.

If you know Gene or meet him at some point, you will agree, I am sure, that *Loudoun Discovered* is delivered in his uniquely informal and casual voice. In fact, as you read these stories you can easily picture Gene sitting by the wood stove in his Waterford office, gathering these tales and exchanging interpretations with local raconteurs. Gene has reminded us that memories, especially those of our wonderful senior citizens, are not always accurate; as we know, different folk will recall the same event differently. This is not a reason, however, for excluding these recollections from a publication such as this. They help amplify the facts and bring these facts to life.

We hope reading these volumes will stimulate you to do some further digging into the history of this beautiful and historic county. The very best place to do that, bar none, is the Thomas Balch Library in Leesburg. It is a great place to carry out your research.

Enjoy!

Fred Morefield, President
The Friends of the Thomas Balch Library Inc.

Leesburg, Virginia
October 2002

Introduction

Rarely in times past did anyone speak of *eastern* Loudoun. We always called the area lower Loudoun, and that region also included the Aldie and Middleburg neighborhoods. Rather, when you drove east from Leesburg, you'd say you were "goin' down the country," for that area was the least populated in the county.

The term eastern Loudoun slowly became parlance in the mid- and late 1960s, when Sterling Park, the county's first major small-lot subdivision, was being built. Did the settlers of Sterling Park dislike the name "lower Loudoun" because of its possible connotation of inferiority? One does not know. But newspapers began using the term that is now commonplace.

Old eastern Loudoun—save for the Aldie and Middleburg areas—was basically old Broad Run Magisterial District, the vast region east of Goose Creek and present U. S. Route 15. Like all of Loudoun's magisterial districts, it was created in 1870 and was named after the stream that drains much of the region. Before 1870, when for the first time citizens of each district elected their own supervisor, the districts were ruled by court-appointed officials. Perhaps ruled is too strong a term. They were really overseers, who appointed citizens to take care of the roads, the poor, and other matters. Education was not a concern, as there were no public schools before 1870.

Lower Loudoun—if I may call it that—was an area of large farms that had once been parts of even larger plantations. If you look at any map of the county drawn before 1975 and note the public roads, they are fewer and farther apart than the roads that crisscross upper Loudoun. Fewer roads meant fewer people, big farms, and not enough funds from taxes to build a public-road network that could match those west of Goose Creek, where the soil was more productive.

Asa Moore Janney, who recently died at 94, told me that when he was young he'd accompany wheat-cutting machines that would belch their way down the old Leesburg Pike on their way to cut the crops of lower Loudoun farmers on shares. "When we got enough wheat for a sheaf," he told me, "we'd dance around it and sing, 'A sheaf, a sheaf.'" Now, Asa Moore was exaggerating, because instead of the 20 or so sheaves per acre that could be cut around his native Lincoln, there'd be only a couple per acre "down the country."

Lower Loudouners would have preferred a comparison with Fairfax County to its east, for its soils were comparable to theirs. They also would speak of more than 80 dairy farms that dotted their landscape, most of them within four miles of the old Washington & Old Dominion Railroad, so they could get the early-morning milk cans to the railroad before the product spoiled.

This volume gives some space to two of these farmers, Albert Shaw of Sterling and William Morris Stewart of Ashburn and to those old-timers we might add Fitzhugh Thomas of Tecumseh, a 726-acre spread about as far as one could get from civilization on the Bull Run, well south of Conklin. Mr. Thomas held a U. S. record in 1949. On a one-acre field dressed with nitrate of soda, he recorded a yield of 159 bushels of wheat an acre. A 60-bushel-an-acre yield was considered exemplary.

That an agricultural museum, located decades ago at Paeonian Springs, has just opened as the Loudoun Heritage Farm Museum at Claude Moore Park, is a just tribute to a lost area occupation.

What happened to Tecumseh reflects what happened to most of lower Loudoun. The family-farming operation stopped in 1960 and the land was tenanted out. Fences began to wear. Some fields weren't mowed and began to grow up in eastern red cedars—certainly lower Loudoun's official tree. Barns and tenant houses decayed. Slowly, Tecumseh blended back into the landscape, awaiting the speculator's dollar. Then, years more of waiting for the right time in the economic cycle.

That right time for many came in January 1958, when President Dwight Eisenhower put Washington Dulles International Airport in the midst of Down the Country. By the time of the airport's opening in November 1962, water and sewer lines had been laid, new and wider roads were being planned and built, and Marvin Broyhill's brain was toying with Sterling Park. What followed in ensuing decades merely echoed that first controversy: Should "The Park" be built, or shouldn't it be built? It would be at least four decades of sparring between eastern Loudoun and western Loudoun.

Eugene Scheel
June 2002

EASTERN
LOUDOUN

0   1   2   3   4
MILES

0 1 2 3 4 5 6 7
KILOMETERS

🏠 🏠 🏚 Standing Historic Buildings, not in Original Use
∴ No-Longer-Standing Historic Buildings
------- Old Public Roads
———— Post-1960 Roads
Historic Road Names in Parentheses

Cot
ROUTE 7
1st Belmont Sch
Crest Belmont
Trap Rock
Belmonta
Belmont Parke
Be
STUBBLE ROAD
Ch
2nd Belmont School
Graves
GOOSE
ALEXANDRIA (WASHINGTON) ROAD
BELMONT RIDGE
HAY ROAD
ASHBU
Murray's Ford
Ashburn Farm
SHELLHORN
DULLES
Evergreen Mills Creek
BELMONT
Broad Run Church
WAXPOOL ROAD
ROAD
Beaverda
Alh
Hard
WAXPOOL
Reservoir
Goose
River
Negro Mountain
RESERVOIR RD
MOUNT HOPE RD
Mount Hope Church
WAXPOOL
Mount Hope School
BEAVERDAM
Little
Branch
ROAD
Black Branch
2nd Red Hill School
EVERGREEN
CROSEN LANE
BELMONT RIDGE
Watson Mountain Church
WATSON
RED HILL ROAD
TOM
RYAN
ROAD
RYAN
R
First Baptist Church
1st Red Hill School
ROAD
Brambleton School
HIGHWAY
U.S. ROUTE 15
Owsley's
CAROLINA
Peggy's Green
MILLS
Royville
CREIGHTON
Broad
ROAD
Gilbert's Corner
LOUDOUN BRANCH
FLEETWOOD ROAD (SMITH'S ROAD)
2nd Cameron Parish Glebe
BELMONT ROAD
OLD
ROAD
CARTE
U.S. 50
MONROE
JOHN
MOSBY
LENAH
OF THE
ARCOLA
(CARCOLA ROAD)
Mount Zion Church
ROAD
RACEFIELD LANE
MANASS
West's Ordinary
Lenah School
Toll House
3rd Arcola School
JAMES
BRADDOCK
Hutchison's Mill
1st Arcola P.O.
Glascock Field
VANCE
U.S. RO
Little River Church
ROAD
LENAH
ROAD
(SMITH'S
GOSHEN ROAD)
(LITTLE RIVER TURNPIKE)
HIGHWAY
OX ROAD
NEW
ROAD
PEACH ORCHARD LANE
(COLCHESTER
ROAD)
Goshen (house)
Corner Hall
LIGHTRIDGE FARM ROAD (CATHARPIN ROAD)
Goshen
2nd Shiloh Church
GUM SPRING
ELK LICK RD. (CONKLIN ROAD)
Pleasant Valley Scho
PLEASANT
Bull Run
PRINCE WILLIAM COUNTY
CHEETINGHOUSE LA.)
(SMITH'S
ROAD)
(GOSHEN ROAD)
Lunette
Pleasant Valley

Goshen

Goshen, a Hebrew word meaning mound of earth, is an apropos name for the corner of the old Colchester and Leesburg Roads. The area is still earthen, right down to its travelways. And like that biblical land of Goshen in the eastern Nile Delta, it is grazing country.

Before the corner was named Goshen, it was known as "The Post." The Post had its genesis shortly after 1768. That same year, Benjamin Franklin, first postmaster general of the American Colonies, began a packet mail line along the main coastal roads between Falmouth, Massachusetts and Charleston, South Carolina. One of the mail stops was on King's Highway at the Fairfax County seaport of Colchester. From Colchester, more-informal and less-regular carriers brought the mails west. Their first stop was in Loudoun County at The Post.

At The Post, where there is still not a house in sight, horses, wagons, and carts stopped. Mails for Leesburg went north, those for Prince William County went south, and mails for other points continued west on the Colchester Road, across the Blue Ridge to Winchester and beyond.

"The Post" primarily referred to the mail stop, but there was also the all-important directional post. Ordered by the county court, the local overseer of the road set up such posts at important intersections. Here, the post might have read: "Leesburg 14 miles; Winchester 42 miles," with possibly an addition to the latter direction noting "West's Ordinary 3 miles." In 1768 there were no villages in between.

Nor were there any in 1801, when Goshen Post Office marked the corner. It was the first post office in lower Loudoun, and the fourth in the county, following Leesburg (1793), Middleburg (1798), and Waterford (1800). Aldie's William Cooke, who in 1809 would co-own the Aldie Mill with Charles Fenton Mercer, was the first postmaster, and he probably picked the name Goshen—a reference to the land where Joseph, prime minister of Egypt, settled the Israelites (Gen. 46).

The mill, largest manufactory in Loudoun, was the western terminus of the Little River Turnpike, which was completed in 1809. This toll road paralleled the Colchester Road, running just two miles north of the old travelway. The new turnpike was straight as an arrow and paved with rock; two vehicles could pass each other on it with neither having to pull over into the muck. Despite its tolls, the turnpike began to take traffic away from the older road. The new road was managed by Quaker Phineas Janney, a frugal business executive. Under his direction, the Little River became one of few Virginia turnpikes to show a profit. By 1821 traffic on the Colchester Road had declined so much that the last Goshen postmaster, Lewis M. Smith, closed the office that August.

In its heyday Goshen appeared on one map, the Carey-Lea Map of Virginia, engraved in Philadelphia, circa 1810. Had the name not been on that map, the location of Goshen might have been lost. Yardley Taylor, chronicling Loudoun settlements in Joseph Martin's 1835 *Gazetteer of Virginia*, still listed Goshen as "a small village in the southern part of the county, about 35 ms. W. of W.," the latter phrase meaning west of Washington.

By mid-century another corner, a half-mile west of Goshen on the old Colchester Road, came into area prominence as Corner Hall. Here, a meeting hall had been built. At times, some say, it was used as a tavern. The building site vanished before anyone now can recall.

Goshen was still a name in general use, though. In fact, on May 28, 1853, when Harrison and Catharine Cross sold a small farm to their newly married daughter Julia Ann Frances and her husband Robert Poland, the parcel was named Goshen, even though it lay a mile and a half northwest of the original village. The Crosses sold 112 acres for $63.72 "in consideration for the natural love and affection" they felt for their daughter.

PHOTO BY JAMES BIRCHFIELD
COURTESY LOUDOUN TIMES-MIRROR

Goshen, the 1890s Sewell Polen House

Four days earlier, the Crosses had bought the same 112 acres for $1,327. Thus began a new Goshen.

According to Harriett Polen Ellison, her uncle Sewell Polen built the present beaded-clapboard, twin-stone-chimneyed dwelling in the 1890s. An earlier house dated from the 1850s. A cornerstone of the newer dwelling presents the following hieroglyphics:

Even holding the characters up to a mirror doesn't make sense out of most of them.

$$\wedge \forall : \Gamma \sqsubset \text{i} \text{I} : C H \forall \; 18 \ell \Gamma$$

By 1888 the name Goshen no longer appeared in deeds, and the Colchester Road was called the "old Braddock Road," a misdirected tribute to W. H. Snowden, who had incorrectly interpreted the route that John Dalrymple outlined in his orderly books about British Major General Edward Braddock's ill-fated expedition to Fort Duquesne.

By 1910 the cabin of Lewis Smith, last Goshen postmaster, crumbled. The site, outlined by a grove of trees, is some 60 feet northwest of The Post, or Goshen, corner. Only the Smith name remains: old-timers now call Fleetwood Road, Smith's Road.

Arcola

Formerly Gum Spring; Before That, Springfield

In 1882 an Arcola old-timer told a visiting journalist that the oldest building in town had been constructed 140 years before. It may have been the survivor of two businesses, a distillery and a pot house, that had stood by Broad Run and the Gum Spring. The pot house—a kiln complex for baking brick—stood 500 feet east of the village. In 1796 the structure was known as a bake house that Matthew Franklin Bowne & Company had built. One year later a chancery suit noted that Henry Banks and Robert Smock had bought the distillery adjacent to the bake house. In 1835 the distillery was still operating but the kilns were a memory.

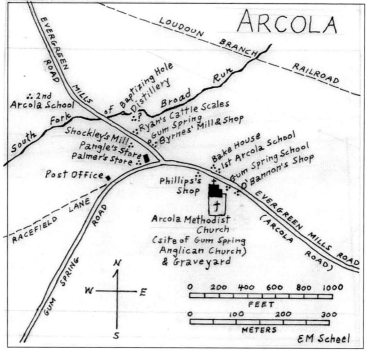

Near the Gum Spring, which through the 1960s bubbled up at five gallons a minute, stood an Anglican Church named for the spring. The church, which was probably log, is labeled "Gum Spring Meeting house" on a circa 1778 map of Loudoun.

In 1854 the Reverend William Meade, Virginia's venerable Episcopal bishop, wrote in his personal recollections of colonial Anglican churches in *Old Churches, Ministers and Families in Virginia:*

> In the year 1758 the Rev. John Andrews was its minister; whether before or after this, or how long, is not known. . . In the years 1773, 1774, and 1776, the Rev. Spence Grayson was the minister; whether before or after, or how long, is not known. There was a church in it [Cameron Parish] near the Gumspring, the traces of which are yet to be seen.

The church's traces had disappeared by 1882. However, the Cameron Parish Glebe, built about 1748 and the oldest of the grand houses of lower Loudoun, still stands, two and a half miles northwest of Arcola. The land, initially 1,746 acres, had been granted to "the Rev. Doctor Charles Green" in 1740, for his farm. The word *glebe* derives from *gleba,* the Latin word for soil or earth. Each colonial Anglican parish gave glebe land to its parson and then built a house for him on the land. Citizens' taxes paid for the land and dwelling.

The Reverend Dr. Green, a physician as well as a parson, named his tract Peggy's Green, as Peggy was the pet name for his wife, Margaret. Despite controversies regarding his many reported infidelities, which included the seduction of teenage daughters of parishioners, Dr. Green served as Cameron Parish parson from 1731 to 1761. As a physician he attended George and Martha Washington. George's father, Captain Augustine Washington, had recommended Dr. Green for his first parish position at Truro, Fairfax County.

In 1761 the Greens sold part of their farm, including the house tract, to politician William Ellzey. The eastern 600 acres of Peggy's Green remained the Cameron Parish Glebe, and on it a new house (no longer standing) was built for the next parson, the Reverend Spence Grayson. This house, noted in 1774 as standing, was not occupied by Reverend Grayson for long. By 1776 he was a chaplain in his brother's Continental regiment. In 1802 the Virginia General Assembly divested the old Anglican Church of its glebe lands, giving them to the county Overseers of the Poor. Three years later the overseers sold the property to Francis H. Peyton.

Presbyterian Church records note that by 1776 the Reverend Amos Thompson, a Princeton-educated missionary, was holding services at the Gum Spring Church. He had founded the Catoctin Presbyterian

Church, two miles south of Waterford, in 1764 and soon held services at another former Anglican church, Broad Run, just east of Waxpool. The independently wealthy Reverend Thompson lived on 755 acres near present-day Evergreen Mills, which he purchased from William Grayson, the regimental commander whose brother, the Reverend Spence Grayson, had been Thompson's ministerial predecessor. Like Grayson, Thompson also served as an army chaplain. By 1781, the Leesburg-born Reverend David Bard was the Presbyterian minister at Gum Spring. He later left Loudoun, turned politician, and was elected to the U. S. Congress from Pennsylvania, 1795-1815.

During this era, Gum Spring Church was a "Free Church," open to all Christian denominations. It may still have been in use in 1816, for a plat of its graveyard locates the headstone of Cornelius Wyckoff, 1760-1816. The headstone is just east of the present Methodist Church, which was built about 1853 in the middle of the old Gum Spring grave-yard. The churchyard was then known as the "schoolhouse lot" or the "graveyard lot." The Methodists used the church two Sabbaths a month, and other denominations worshipped there on the remaining Sabbaths. One can still see depressions of the graveyard of 200 years past, and the base of the one remaining tombstone in the border of a rock garden. In 1835 when Loudoun geographer Yardley Taylor described the community, he did not mention a church:

> Arcola is Gum Spring, a small village containing eight dwelling houses, two mercantile stores, one tanyard, one blacksmith shop and a distillery. Population 20. This section of country is thickly settled though the land is generally poor.

Mr. Taylor's population estimate was incorrect, however, for the average family size was then about five.

A post office named Springfield had been in the village from 1801 to 1819, probably to serve the bake house and distillery. The office, manned by postmaster Stephen Bayard, was the fifth-oldest in Loudoun County and the second-oldest in lower Loudoun. U. S. postal records incorrectly note its location as Fairfax County. In 1798 the current Loudoun-Fairfax line, two miles east of Arcola, was surveyed, and as geography was then quite hazy, Bayard's explanation of his post office's location placed it in Fairfax. Virginia post office records, however, note Springfield's location as Loudoun.

That the next post office was not in the village that Yardley Taylor described was due to the success of the Little River Turnpike, today's Route 50. From 1832 to 1868 this first "Arcola" Post Office was located at a still-standing stucco-and-log home with stone chimneys, just north of the Arcola Elementary School, on the south side of the old turnpike. The house was the seat of Matthew P. Lee's 540-acre Arcola Farm, hence the new post office's name, which has no apparent meaning. Springfield could no longer be used as a post office name, because by 1832 there was a Springfield in Hampshire County. Gum Spring was out of the question because Lee's post office was two miles away from the spring and because in 1836 a Gum Spring Post Office had been established in Amelia County.

People walked or rode from the village to the Arcola Post Office on Racefield Lane, still a public road in the 1930s when it had the route number 298. The lane ran down the middle of the three-quarter-mile oval track of the Arcola Racefield. Back in the late 19th century, Lady Melba (named for the Australian soprano Nellie Melba), owned by the Everharts, and Sir Dick, owned by the Bradshaws, ran some of their greatest races here. The races stopped about 1910.

In the early 1850s the construction gang of the Loudoun Branch of the Manassas Gap Railroad camped at Gum Spring. The bed they graded can still be seen 1,000 feet north of the village between two rows of trees. Tracks were actually laid to this point—some say as far as Route 15—but were dismantled by Confederates when they abandoned their perimeter around Washington in the fall of 1861. The Loudoun Branch was to connect Harper's Ferry with the Manassas Gap's main line near Centreville in Fairfax County, but the Panic of 1857 ended the railroad's hope, and the Virginia Legislature failed to come through with supplementary funds.

Some 40 percent of the Arcola area's population in the 1850s was black, and nearly all of the Negroes were slaves. A vestige of the era survives in a five-room stone slave quarters on the old Lewis farm just east of the village. Here, Charles and Thomas B. Lewis housed more than a dozen slaves. The quarters, one of Virginia's notable remaining examples of this genre, has been proffered to the county government and will soon be restored.

That the citizenry of old Gum Spring voting precinct, which comprised nearly all of southeast Loudoun, favored slavery, was indicated on May 23, 1861, in its 135-5 vote to secede from the Union. The Virginia Legislature had already voted, 88-55, to secede and thought its decision important enough to bring the issue to a popular vote.

Matthew Lee remained the Arcola postmaster under both the Union and the Confederacy, through 1865. But as a Southerner, he was replaced after the conflict. Still, the post office remained at his house by the Little River Turnpike until 1868. Then, members of the Methodist Church asked the U. S. Post Office to move the Arcola Post Office to the village.

Lewis Farm slave quarters, before restoration

Businesses of the 1870s and 1880s were dominated by the general merchandise store of L. F. Palmer, at the site of the present-day Pangle's Store, and by the store of Philip F. VanSickler (at a location that isn't known). Through 1915, as the White House shifted from a Republican to a Democrat, so the Arcola Post Office shifted from a "Republican" store to a "Democrat" store. By 1884 Jefferson Davis Lambert operated a general store in competition with L. F. Palmer's. Lemuel O'Bannon was a coach-and wagon-maker with a shop just east of the church.

The village had four physicians during these four-or-so decades, E. L. Turner, J. E. Warner, Frederick Hutchison, and J. D. Lambert. In the 1890s J. D. Lambert, who was tired of running his store, joined Frederick Hutchison's practice. Dr. Fred's cousin, Claudius P. Hutchison, took over the practice about 1900, and a kissing cousin, Hugh B. Hutchison, was the village dentist during the 1890s. The Hutchisons' house and office stood south of the present Pangle's Store and burned in the 1920s.

In the early 1890s brothers Will and Litt Byrne started a gasoline-powered mill by the spring. Litt was a master mechanic and millwright (he also had a sawmill in Chantilly), and his brother was a blacksmith. Together they ran a wheelwright and blacksmith shop by the mill, which they had taken over from Curtis Ambler, husband of Olivia Ambler, the Aldie telephone-switchboard operator. Litt kept a "Bachelor's Hall" room—for cardplayers—above the mill, and across the road was a creamery. In the early teens the Byrnes moved their mill and shop east of the church, to the old O'Bannon house and shop. Their shop closed in the late 1920s; their mill in 1938. The structures came down in 1950.

Between the Byrne brothers' first shop and the Gum Spring Church stood Murray D. Philips's blacksmith shop, in operation from about 1900. Mr. Murray specialized in sharpening tools and blades for the highway department. He was puttering around until 1945. Behind the shop, during the World War I years and the 1920s, his son, Gilbert Philips had a garage, where he repaired Model Ts. The Methodist Church bought the property, tore down the buildings, and built a parsonage on the site.

Walter L. Palmer ran his family's Arcola store during the 1890s, but moved the business to Pleasant Valley in the early 20th century. His old store was taken over first by George Henry Shryock and then by Charles J. C. Maffett about 1905. Besides general merchandise, Mr. Maffett featured hardware and furniture. Around 1908 competition came from C. W. "Billy" Barton and J. W. Pearson's Store, located just east of the Byrnes' first mill. Messrs. Barton and Pearson sold out to Charles A. "Charlie" Whaley and Arch Mankin in the mid-teens. Mr. Mankin ran the store un-til it became a Depression ca-sualty about 1935. Several of these businesses, notably Mr. Mankin's, were financed by the Virginia general assemblyman

Pangle's Store still thrives in Arcola

and cattle and land dealer John F. Ryan, whose cattle scales were west of the Gum Spring. Mr. Ryan made money by saving money, carrying a bag lunch to the directors' meetings at Peoples National Bank in Leesburg. What is now Pangle's Store, one of the three old village groceries in eastern

The former Shockley's Mill, once home of "Flavo Arcola Flour"

Loudoun, started after Mr. Mankin and Mr. Whaley parted company. Charlie Whaley built the store in 1921 and ran it until 1946. The store housed the post office from 1923 until 1946, when Leslie "Les" Pangle took over the grocery. He still owns the business but since 1992 has leased it to Jim Schottler. Mr. Schottler's stuffed-animal and-bird collections embellish the grocery's interior.

Vying for the Byrne brothers' milling trade, Virgil Walker built a two-and-a-half-story frame mill west of Pangle's Store in 1917. Jay C. Shockley ran the mill from 1925, with its two burrs (millstones) grinding corn into meal and wheat into flour until 1955. A 40-hp engine, started with gasoline and run by kerosene, turned the machinery. The mill's fancy flour bags bore the lettering "Flavo Arcola Flour." The mill was in decrepit condition when youngsters burned it down in 1980.

By 1909 the post office had settled in Charles Maffett's Store, but in 1915, Ann Middleton Orrison became postmistress and moved the office to a small building by her house. Before her tenure of some 18 years, 15 postmasters and postmistresses had held the job since 1865—an average of one every three and a half years. In 1946 the post office moved to a 1933 store owned by Jay Shockley. His daughter Mary Virginia Shockley served as postmistress until 1952, when she gave the job to her mother, Rachel Shockley. Rachel held the position until 1975, when her daughter again took over, this time for 20 years. "About seven [postmistresses] have followed," Mary Shockley told me recently. Rachel and Jay Shockley ran the store until it closed in 1981.

Arcola's first public school was a frame one-roomer built around 1880. After closing in 1908 it was used as the post office for a year or so, and then became the Barton-Pearson Store. The structure was torn down in the late 1970s when a new house was built near it. The owner of the house still uses the school pump for water. The second school, also a one-roomer, with a front porch and the date "1910" inscribed over the door, stood on a knoll about 1,000 feet west of the South Fork of Broad Run, on the south side of Evergreen Mills Road. It served until 1939, when it was torn down. Eugene Ferne Marshall's house replaced it after World War II.

The last building of note to be constructed in Arcola was the handsome brick one-story, six-room Arcola School of 1939, now the community center. It was the only school in Loudoun to be built with federal funds from the Public Works Administration. It closed in 1975, and children in the area now attend the Arcola School that sits just south of the first Arcola Post Office, which Matthew Lee ran from1832 to 1865. Arcola's population in the Centennial Year, 1876, was noted as about 30, and a 1911 business directory lists 90 people in the village. In the Bicentennial Year,1976, the population had grown to what it is today, about 135. Through the 1960s many of Arcola's residents bucketed their potable water from the Gum Spring. Since then the highway department has widened the road so that the spring is hardly visible. Through the 1970s, Leslie Pangle regularly "cleaned it out" and even placed a barrel over it so it would not fill in with debris.

What happened to the the gum tree? A strong wind knocked it over in the early 1950s.

No history of Arcola would be replete without a snippet about Glascock Field, a half mile south. Delmas T. Glascock began laying out the airstrip in 1941, and at close-by Blue Ridge Airport near Willard, started teaching Forest G. "Buddy" Thompson to fly. Then came the war, stifling construction until the close of '45. With the field licensed in July 1946, Buddy, who got his U. S. Air force wings in '43, taught flying at Glascock's Field, and when business slowed down, he'd do acrobatics in his T-19 World War II trainer to attract sightseers at $5 an hour.

Lanesville "The Sisters' Tract"

In its late-18th-and-early-19th-century heyday, Lanesville was a stopping place for travelers along the forerunner of Route 7, the Vestal's Gap Road. Both its hostelry, which served as the second-oldest Loudoun post office east of Broad Run, and the road are in a pristine state—the focal points of today's Claude Moore Park.

Thomas Barnes of Westmoreland County had been granted the land early in 1729, but he died before the deed was recorded. Thus, his three children, Abraham, Elizabeth, and Frances, inherited it later that year. The son's grant for 1,003 acres was the eastern half of the tract. The daughters' grant for 1,003 acres was the western half, and it became known as "The Sisters' Tract," described simply as "on Broad Run of Potomac." Upon this tract a Lanesville house, built in sections from about 1770 to about 1810, arose.

The road prompted the house and a probable earlier dwelling on that same site or close by. In the mid-1700s the road was known by a number of names. Sometimes it was called the Eastern Ridge Road because it crossed the Blue Ridge 27 miles to the west. Often it was called the New Church Road or Upper Church Road because the 1734 Anglican Falls Church stood 16 miles to the east. Potomac Ridge Road and The Great Road were other names. The name Vestal's Gap became common only after 1924, when histo-

PHOTO COURTESY OF LOUDOUN COUNTY DEPT.OF PLANNING

Vestal's Gap Road today,
Claude Moore Park

rian Fairfax Harrison gave it that appellation, for the Route 9 gap in the Blue Ridge, now called by an older name, Keyes' Gap.

When the Fairfax County Courthouse stood at its Tyson's Corner location, 1742-52, the Vestal's Gap Road received heavy traffic, for Loudoun was then a part of Fairfax County. And after being improved in the 1740s, the road became a major westward travelway.

George Washington traveled along the road in early November 1753 and in early April 1754, on his way to the western Pennsylvania outposts of Fort Leboeuf and Fort Necessity. Scots Captain John Dalrymple, who surveyed northern Virginia in 1754, mapped the road's course, first shown on the 1755 edition of the Philip Fry-Peter Jefferson Map of Virginia and Maryland.

In April 1755, British Colonel Sir Peter Halkett's 44th Grenadiers, under the command of Major General Edward Braddock, marched past the Barnes sisters' place on their way to defeat by the French and Indians at Fort Duquesne (today's Pittsburgh). Research by eastern Loudoun historian Carl McIntyre has established that about 65 percent of Braddock's army took this route. General Braddock, however, did not. He went northwest by way of old Route 40 in Maryland. Yet, his fame was such that into the early 20th century, area old-timers would say that the "Braddock Road" went by Lanesville.

Early descriptions of the Sisters' Tract did not mention this main road, but a 1763 deed notes the land contained "Houses out houses Buildings Gardens Orchards Meadows Pastures Trees Waters & Watercourses," on "Stony Hill called the Mountain." A 1777 deed to Hardage Lane for part of the Sisters' Tract nearly repeats that description.

Hardage Lane, a Loudouner, married Rachel Beall of Montgomery County, Maryland, in 1746, and they had eight children. Two became doctors; another, Ninean Edwards, was first territorial governor of Illinois; a daughter, Lydia, married William Coleman, proprietor of a tavern three miles down the road, on the east side of Sugarland Run. The building is long gone, but a family graveyard survives.

After his marriage, Mr. Lane moved to Montgomery County, and he died there in 1803. Three years earlier he had bought the remainder of the Sisters' Tract from his brother, William Lane Sr., who had acquired the land in 1779. When he died, Hardage Lane owned thousands of acres in Loudoun and Montgomery Counties, 21 slaves, and a "ferry-boat" used to ply the Potomac between his holdings. His son Samuel thought it best that his sister Keturah live at Stony Hill.

On December 3, 1803, in Montgomery County, Maryland, Keturah Lane, mistress of Stony Hill, married John Keene. Her sister Lydia Lane Coleman would talk to him about how good business was at their tavern on Sugarland Run, three miles east, so Mr. Keene became convinced that the thing to do was to open an "ordinary"—the popular pre-War of 1812 name for a tavern that served ordinary meals to all comers at a fixed price. From 1799 when Andrew Lane, Hardage's son, kept the Lanesville Ordinary, various family members continued the enterprise for about two decades. And so the appelation "Lanesville."

That name first appeared on April 1, 1807, when John Keene was appointed postmaster of a new village called Lanesville in honor of his wife and her father. Upon Keene's death in 1814 William Palmer took over. When Keturah Lane Keene remarried in 1817, her new husband, Benjamin Bridges, became postmaster. The last mail-sorter, James Bland, took over on December 31, 1821, and after that date the record is incomplete. In all probability, the Lanesville Post Office did not last long beyond 1822. Just one year earlier, 1821, the Leesburg and Georgetown Turnpike (today's Route 7) had been completed a mile to the north. Mail carriers were now riding along the turnpike, where a Whaley's Store Post Office at Broad Run had opened in 1817. The new turnpike also did in the tavern, which had never been as popular as Coleman's, despite its owners' high hopes that it would become the "Half-way House" between Winchester and Washington.

In the early 19th century much of the outlying Barnes land was leased and sold to Sampson Blincoe, just as it had been leased and sold to his father Thomas Blincoe in the second half of the 18th century. In the middle of the Blincoe tract there was the 215-acre Stony Hill, or "Little Mountain," tract of Benjamin Bridges. It became his property on October 10, 1829. On that date, Hardage Lane, grandson of the first Hardage, and wife Rebecca Ann sold Little Mountain to Ben Bridges for $900. Since his marriage to Keturah Keene in 1817, Mr. Bridges had farmed the Sisters' Tract, and through the 1830s he and his wife acquired other sections of the tract from Keturah's brothers James and William.

By the time of the Civil War, Little Mountain, alias Lanesville, alias Stony Hill, was known as the Bridges place. The hill itself was a 442-foot-high eminence, the highest point in Loudoun east of Goose Creek. At its summit was a signal station, and from the station's platform one could observe doings on the Leesburg Turnpike at Belmont, six miles west, and at Dranesville, three miles east.

Signaling was nothing new to area residents. In presidential election years, as soon as the ballots had been counted in Washington, signal fires were lit and their messages relayed by blankets, Indian-style, from hill to hill. By the next morn, news of the election winners had reached the Mississippi River.

Ben Bridges' son, also Benjamin Bridges, was a Dartmouth graduate, who by 1853 had returned to Lanesville. He married Lucy "Elizabeth" Elgin on December 13, 1853, and they had a son, Dorsey Bridges, born at Lanesville in 1854. Ben Bridges Jr. was a Loudoun justice of the peace and a noted Old School Baptist preacher at North Fork, Frying Pan, and Thumb Run Meetinghouses. He also taught boys in a school on the farm.

He was quite nearsighted and thus did not enter the Confederate Army. Nevertheless, he was imprisoned by the Yankees for a year in the old Capitol Street prison in Washington, D. C. The Bridges place was in the middle of a no-man's-land for much of the war: Confederates to the west, Yankees to the east. Marauders often came through, and Bridges family members recall that at one point only an old cow remained. The Bridges hid the cow inside the house, but the Yankees got it anyway.

PHOTO COURTESY OF MARY BREED

Benjamin Bridges' Schoolhouse,
soon to be restored at Claude Moore Park

At the war's end, Benjamin Bridges reopened his private school for boys, which now boarded the students. About 1870 he had a two-story frame school built. The school lasted until 1875, when Mr. Bridges moved to Greenland, his mother's home place in "The Kingdom" neighborhood north of Evergreen Mills. The frame schoolhouse stands today. Remaining at Lanesville was Ben's daughter Irene, who until the 1920s shared the Bridges place with her friend Annie Miskel. Ben Bridges Jr. owned the farm at that time.

In 1900, when he died, his will passed the property to his wife, Lucy Elgin Bridges, who died four years later. To settle her estate, the Bridges place was sold at auction and was bought by Irene Huntington

Bridges, Ben and Lucy's daughter. At auction the farm, then 452 acres, was improved with "frame dwelling, 8 rooms in fair condition. Barn and stabling for six horses and a good well of water at the house." About 100 acres was timbered, "and the whole [was] under fair fencing."

"On the Thursday before Pearl Harbor Sunday 1941," as Dr. Claude Moore tells it, he bought the Bridges place, now 414 acres, at an auction for $16,000. He renamed the farm Lanesmoore.

Dr. Moore's long career, which began after he graduated from the University of Virginia Medical School in 1916, alternated between medicine and real estate. He served as a physician with the U. S. Army in World War I and then joined the Mayo Clinic, where he specialized in treating cancer with radiology. He came to Washington in 1929 as head of the George Washington University School of Medicine's roentgenology (x-ray radiology) department.

Realizing that the federal government was not getting any smaller, Dr. Moore began to invest in real estate. One of his holdings was 1412 16th Street NW in Washington, and in 1938 he helped the National Wildlife Federation to obtain the zoning that would permit it to move into the building. Thus began a long and friendly relationship—Dr. Moore had always been interested in animal life—that led to his donating 357 acres of his farm to the federation in 1974. Dr. Moore described what the farm was like in the early 1940s:

> There was no running water. It had to be carried from a spring, located two good city blocks from the house. Food that had to be kept reasonably cold in summer had to be immersed in that same spring.
>
> There was no electricity and evening chores had to be done by the light of an oil lamp. For warmth and cooking there was an old wood stove, often stubborn and seldom cooperative.
>
> There was no indoor bathroom. The outhouse stood across the road from the home. It was later moved to the barnyard. Overnight guests would frequently tell of the nightmares they had about the outhouse.

He quoted his sister Katherine, who spent many months at the farm each year, as saying, "We felt like pioneer women."

Similar conditions were the norm in most lower Loudoun farmsteads before electricity came in during the late 1940s—courtesy of the

Northern Virginia Electric Cooperative.

Dr. Moore lived at his beloved Lanesmoore until the mid-1980s, well past his 90th birthday. In 1978 he said he was content to know

PHOTO COURTESY OF MARY BREED

Lanesmoore House, Claude Moore Park

that the Wildlife Federation had added ponds and "planned to convert the farm into an educational and conservation center." But in the early 1980s, the federation had financial problems, and in 1986 it reneged on its verbal promise to Dr. Moore and sold Lanesmoore's 357 acres to a developer. Eastern Loudouners and Dr. Moore were outraged, and for four years he tried, without success, to sue the federation for going back on its word. Loudoun's government ended the impasse in 1990 when it floated a bond issue, which voters approved, to buy Lanesmoore. The cost was $13.7 million. The park opened that summer, and the county named its purchase Claude Moore Park to honor the man who had championed the land's preservation. Dr. Moore died the next year at age 99.

Broad Run

**Too Deep
For A Ford;
Too Narrow
For A Ferry**

On April 17, 1699, Broad Run received its name, for Burr Harrison and Giles Vandercastle crossed the stream and wrote in their journals: "About seven or eight miles above the sugar land we came to a broad Branch of about 50 or 60 yards wide: a still or small streeme; it took oure hourses up to the Belleys, very good going in and out."

Mr. Harrison and Mr. Vandercastle had been deputized ambassadors by the Virginia Colony with the purpose to visit the Piscataway Indians, who then lived on Conoy Island, in the Potomac opposite Point of Rocks. The two men led the fourth or fifth known party of Europeans to enter Loudoun. The first and second were David Strahan and his Pottomack Rangers, who explored the Sugarlands area in 1691 and 1692. The third, or possibly fourth, group was Major William Barton and party, who explored unspecified regions to the west in June 1697 and possibly later that year or early in 1698.

The lands at the mouth of Broad Run were first owned by Thomas Lee, for whom Leesburg was named, and Robert Carter Jr., both speculators. Mr. Lee's 460 acres, bought from Thomas, sixth Lord Fairfax, in 1719, were described as "on Broad Run and Lees Creek [Goose Creek] of Potomac River," plus "residue of 340 acres in three islands [Selden's, Van Deventer's, and Ten Foot] in Potomac River above Sugarland [Lowe's] Island." Mr. Carter's holdings to the south were bought in 1731 from Lord Fairfax and totaled 1,498 acres simply noted as "On Broad Run of Potomack" adjacent to Andrew Russell's grant to the west.

On an 1825 deed from Ludwell Lee, who inherited much of his forebear's holdings, the largest of the islands is called "Eden," by legend a transliteration of an unknown Indian name. The buyer that year was cousin Wilson Cary V. Selden, and the island would soon be known by his name. On this island was perhaps the first substantial house in the Broad Run area, a pyramid-roofed brick structure of the Tidewater style. It had been built in the early 1800s for one of the overseers of Lee lands, and it was possibly the only home of the Virginia Lees in Maryland. I understand the structure, in a fine condition 20 years ago, is now a ruin.

In their journals, Harrison and Vandercastle noted that they generally kept a mile from the Potomac, but their exact crossing place is not known. By the late 1730s, however, there was a well-defined horseback trail crossing Broad Run, and mid-century surveys place the crossing point of this trail at the apex of the large horseshoe bend, a half-mile downstream from where Route 7 now crosses the run.

The trail widened to a road that had several names. It was sometimes called the Potomac Ridge Road, or the Eastern Ridge Road, for 25 miles to the west it crossed the Blue Ridge. In 1742 it was called the New Church Road, and in 1755 the Upper Church Road. Both names were for the 1734 Falls Church, as the road passed by that church 18 miles to the east. Many deeds called it the Great Road, a common appellation for major ways in the 18th century, and in Loudoun, after 1924, it was often named the Vestal's Gap Road for the 895-foot high Blue Ridge Gap, where the Charles Town Pike breaches the ridge.

Broad Run was too deep for a ford and too narrow for a ferry, and in the early 1750s a bridge spanned the run. Though bridges were rarities in colonial Virginia, the Fairfax Court felt the span was warranted as its courthouse was located at present-day Tyson's Corner from 1742 to 1752, and thus the Vestal's Gap Road carried a huge load of traffic.

George Washington traveled over or through Broad Run in early November 1753 and in early April 1754, en route to Fort Leboeuf (near Waterford, Pennsylvania) and Fort Necessity, Pennsylvania. His Scots officer, John Dalyrmple, who surveyed the road in 1754, passed over Broad Run and inscribed the words "Woodn Br." on the 1755 edition of the Fry and Jefferson Map of Virginia and Maryland. On April 13, 1755, British Colonel Sir Peter Halkett and a raggle-taggle regiment of Major General Edward Braddock's army crossed the bridge. Sir Peter and his 44th Grenadiers, mainly former convicts and non-landholders forcibly enlisted by the Fairfax County sheriff, were en route to Fort Duquesne (near Pittsburgh)—and a July 9, 1755, defeat by the French and Indians.

Irish poet Thomas Moore described Virginia bridges of that era as "Made of a few uneasy planks / In open ranks / Over rivers of mud." At Broad Run, there were three or four logs, called sleepers, linking each bank. The sleepers supported logs, or boards, called rafters, often not nailed, which were laid at right angles to the sleepers. If the bridge had been flooded by a freshet (fresh), the crosser would have to readjust the rafters and sometimes replace those washed downstream. Such replacements may account for stories told by Broad Run area old-timers that George Washington built the Broad Run Bridge.

When repairs were major, the county court had to provide funds to keep the bridge open, and several entries in 18th-century Loudoun Court minute books note repairs to the bridge. Typical is a 1771 order specifying, "build a bridge at the usual place over Broad Run for £150." That cost may have been equivalent to $500 then, or $50,000 in today's inflationary economy.

Toward the close of the century, Loudoun millers and farmers began to pressure their state legislators for improved roads so they could swiftly move their produce to Alexandria. The Napoleonic Wars in Europe had bred famine, and grain commanded high prices at sea-ports. In 1809, the Virginia Legislature appropriated $41,450 to build the Leesburg Turnpike, 20 miles from Leesburg to Dranesville. The grant was the Commonwealth's largest allocation for building a road. Next year the legislature authorized the sale of 1,000 shares of stock, at $150 a share, in the Leesburg Turnpike Company. The road was advertised to be a right-of-way of 60 feet wide, 17 feet to be covered with gravel or stone, with an additional 17 feet to be cleared and kept open as a "summer road" for horses and walkers. The summer road was also taken when you wanted to pass a slow vehicle.

Tollgates were permitted every five miles; the tolls were specified:
Each horse, mare, mule or gelding, three cents
Two-wheeled riding carriages (carts), 6 ¼ cents.
Four-wheeled riding carriages, 12 ½ cents.
Cart or wagon with wheels not exceeding four inches diameter, three cents per animal.
Every score (20) of sheep or hogs, six cents.
Every score of cattle, 12 ½ cents.
Cart or wagon with wheels between four and seven inches diameter, 1 ½ cents per animal.
Cart or wagon with wheels exceeding seven inches diameter, one cent per animal.

Even though large wheels tore up the road, the cheaper rate encouraged four-and six-horse teams to use the new turnpike instead of the competing Little River Turnpike (now Route 50), 11 miles south.

Sometime before 1809 the main road west had moved to its present location at Broad Run, and in 1810, Levi Whaley, anticipating an improved road, bought 51 acres "on both sides of the turnpike and along Broad Run" for $500. The seller was Henry B "Light Horse Henry" Lee, a Revolutionary hero and former governor of Virginia, who was then heavily in debt. Levi Whaley soon established a store, built a mill, and in 1817 became postmaster of a short-lived post office called Whaley's Store, which closed in 1819.

The one person who claimed to know when the Broad Run Bridge was built was the anonymous writer of Tour 13, Alexandria to Winchester in the 1940 *Guide to the Old Dominion* (the "WPA Writers' Guide"). He noted, "Broad Run Bridge, 27.3 m., carrying the highway on its humped back across the stream here, was built in 1820, according to a date on one of its massive stone buttresses." The tollhouse, still stand-

PHOTO COURTESY OF MURIEL SPETZMAN

The Broad Run Bridge and Toll House in 1952

ing alongside the bridge ruins, dates from the time of the bridge's completion.

Levi Whaley's son, William, sold the mill lot and six acres to Elijah Peacock for $1,366 in 1841. The price suggested the presence of a sawmill. Ten years later, the same property, with a sawmill and a grist-mill, passed to John Jones for only $1,000. The mill stood a few yards north of the westbound lane of Route 7 on the left (west) bank of Broad Run, and was one of five Loudoun mills known to exist at that time east of Goose Creek and Little River. In 1854, Mr. Jones was named postmaster of a new post office at the Broad Run crossing. His store was located 50 yards west of the mill, on the pike. The new post office bore the name Broad Run, and a year later confusion started when the Broad Run Station Post Office (now called Broad Run) opened in Fauquier County.

John Miskel farmed 755 acres at the present Broad Run Farms during these times. On April 1, 1863, one of Colonel John Singleton Mosby's most memorable battles took place at Mr. Miskel's barnyard, where the Confederate colonel and his men had encamped for the night.

In his 1887 *War Reminiscences,* Colonel Mosby wrote,

> Although it was the last day of March, snow was still lying on the ground, and winter lingered on the banks of the Potomac. My authority over the men was of such a transitory nature that I disliked to order them to do anything but fight. Hence I did not put out my pickets on the pike. The enemy's camps were about 15 miles below [near Tyson's Corner, a four-hour horseback journey], and I did not think they could possibly hear of us before the next morning.

Mosby was wrong, for an informer told the Federal troops of the encampment at Miskel's farm. At daybreak, into the barnyard swarmed Union cavalry, "so sure of their prey," wrote Mosby, "that they shut the gates after passing through, in order to prevent any of us from escaping." Colonel Mosby had 70 men, "with more than half unprepared for a fight," and the Federals had 150. In his *Reminiscences,* Mosby stated that he was "surrounded by at least four times our number." But he failed to mention that he had superior firepower against, in many cases, sabers. And so "the combat was short, sharp, and decisive. In the first moment of collision they wheeled and made for the gate which they had already closed against themselves."

Mosby then chased the First Vermont Cavalry five miles down the Leesburg Pike into Dranesville, taking 83 prisoners and 95 horses. There were 23 Union casualties, and Mosby lost 6 men. Knowing the Yankees in Fairfax would soon be in full pursuit, Mosby pulled back, an action

Federal dispatches noted as "He fell back in great haste."

In 1895, New York artist James E. Taylor reconstructed the Miskel's farm fight in an engraving prepared for James J. Williamson's book, *Mosby's Rangers*, and pinpointed its location on Dairy Lane. Pictured by Mr. Taylor, but no longer there, are the rear wall of the Miskel home, burned about 1905; the barn, taken down in 1925; and the pyramid-roof wellhouse, which burned in the late 1960s. A

ILLUSTRATION COURTESY THOMAS BALCH LIBRARY

The fight at Miskel's farm

historical marker, incorrectly dating the fight as March 31, 1863, memorializes the location.

At war's end, Harriet A. Peacock became Broad Run postmistress. With the final closing of the post office on August 9, 1869, the mails shifted to Daysville, two miles east. The post office probably closed because the mill stopped grinding during the war, or shortly afterward.

In 1880, Broad Run settlement passed from the Jones and Peacock families and into the hands of Isaac Van Deventer, who purchased the six-acre mill lot for $120. Mr. Van Deventer also took over Mr. Miskel's farm, operated before and after the war by Mr. Miskel's cousin, Sam Jenkins, and a two-mile-long Potomac island known as Gassaway's, named after the family who owned it most of the 19th century. The Van Deventers owned the island for about 50 years, and the island still bears the Van Deventer name.

Broad Run's first public school dated from the late 1870s and was located at the westbound lane of Route 7 about an eighth of a mile east of Broad Run Drive. The one-room, frame school closed in 1922, with two of its later memorable teachers being Helen Collier and Margaret Franklin. A decade after the closing, the school was moved to Sterling Farm, where it housed farmhands until it fell in, a decade or so ago.

In 1866 the state of Virginia got out of the turnpike business, and many of the state-owned Loudoun turnpikes, including the Leesburg Pike, were transferred to privately owned stock companies. Leesburg Pike by this time was a rough 14-foot-wide cobblestone affair, its holes filled with sawdust from the many lumber mills between the road and the Potomac River.

Before the 1920s, the bulk of traffic on the Leesburg Pike was made up of four- and six-horse team wagons, piled high with two to three tons of loose hay (no balers, then). Hickory boom poles held down each layer of hay. You would load a layer at a time, then boom it down. Each layer weighed about a ton. The teams were decked out with bells in their bridles, with the lead team's bells pitched a few notes higher. The horses were mostly Percherons and some Clydesdales. With practice, one could recognize the teams before they came into view by their clinking and clanging.

On the way to the District or Alexandria, the wagoners stopped for the night at the Dranesville Tavern, paying 25 cents for lodging, with no charge for parking. Next morning they would be at their desti-

nation, with the wagons greeted by poor blacks, who would unload the wagons in return for the 25-foot-long hickory boom poles, ideal for firewood. The farmers got $25 a ton for their hay, sold mostly to livery stables and to horsecar and fire engine companies. Returning to Loudoun, the wagoners again spent 25 cents for a night at Dranesville Tavern and made it back home the next day.

During the post-Civil War years and into the 1920s, Broad Run at the old mill pond by the stone bridge was the choice site for winter ice—Sugarland and Difficult Runs being the other possibilities—

PHOTO COURTESY LOUDOUN CO. PLANNING DEPT.

A forgotten grave stone and remains of Broad Run village

because its five-foot-deep waters produced ice that could be hacked away in three-foot blocks by handsaw and ax.

After the Civil War tolls were sporadically collected at the Leesburg Pike station by Broad Run. Because of financial troubles, the turnpike company often had to close the tollgate and cease road repairs. In 1911 banker Robert Harper of Caradoc Hall, east of Leesburg, organized the Washington Good Roads Association, bought the turnpike franchise, and reinstated the toll at 25 cents for an auto and 10 cents for a horse-and-wagon team. There was no charge for a horse-and-rider or a walker; ministers and physicians traveled free; and tolls were not collected on Sunday, when it was assumed that all travelers were going to or from church.

Amos Jenkins, a proprietor of a hotel called the Ashburn House, lived near the Broad Run Tollhouse and farmed the acreage about; some of his tenants were the last tollkeepers. During World War I, bootlegger Lerttie Holsinger, rumored to have killed more than one man, partnered with Amos Jenkins and sold homemade whiskey (remembered as "real hot stuff") for $2 a pint and $8 or $9 a gallon from Jenkins' small stone house (the former miller's cottage) that stood west of the run until the early 1960s. Their operation was classed as a "jump-about proposition": here one day, gone the next.

In the early 1920s the partners got into an argument, and Holsinger killed Jenkins with a .22. The killing stopped sales of bootleg at the run for a while. Curtis Jenkins and Ralph Cochran kept traffic turning to the river on Miskel's Lane with a good-sized still operation on Van Deventer's Island. Their output, though, never matched the magnitude (or taste) of Earl Batt's still production on Ten Foot Island. But by the end of Prohibition in 1933, the only business left at Broad Run was at the tollhouse, as its gardens to the rear were open to visitors for 10 cents—for a view of the "sturdy bridgeside." By then the bootleggers, most of whom were named Jenkins, sold their brew at the tollhouse.

In 1924 the tolls came off the pike, and the road officially became Route 54 of the new state highway network. Because of the bumpy and rutted condition of the road, however, travelers east continued to prefer going south on Route 15 and east on Route 50, both smooth macadamized roads. It was not until 1929 that Route 7 east of Leesburg was paved, and it was not until 1940 or so that the travel patterns changed.

In 1945 the Virginia highway department wanted to tear down the stone Broad Run Bridge and build a new road and bridge in the same place. Properly incensed, the Leesburg Garden Club protested, and for its efforts to preserve the bridge was awarded the Massie Medal, the highest honor bestowed by the Virginia Garden Club. And so the new concrete-and-steel bridge, its plaque bearing the date 1948, was built a few feet to the north. Unfortunately, the highway department did not tell the Garden Club that the old bridge would need repointing and bracing, at a cost, then, of some $5,000. The bridge was never repaired or braced, and when Tropical Storm Agnes came along in June 1972, the floods in its wake washed away the west span; the bridge's total collapse came on February 19, 1976. The tollhouse survives.

Ruins of the Broad Run Bridge, post-Tropical Storm Agnes

Belmont

Ludwell Lee's "Beautiful Mountain"

Belmont is one of four Loudoun plantations that evolved into villages: the others; New Lisbon, Oatlands, Woodburn. Its beginnings trace to grants totaling 11,182 acres from Thomas, sixth Lord Fairfax, to Thomas Lee, between 1719 and 1728. Tenants planted corn and tobacco on this land, ranging from Broad Run to Goose Creek, which Thomas Lee liked to call Lee's Creek. In part, the land passed to Thomas's seventh son, Richard Henry Lee, signer of the Declaration of Independence, and then to Richard Lee's second son, Ludwell Lee, born in 1760 to the former Ann Aylett, at Chantilly, Westmoreland County.

Ludwell Lee gave the Belmont manor house, built 1800-1803, its name, French for "beautiful mountain." The manor was aptly named, for it rests near the top of a 415-foot-high ridge, soon to take the name of its manor.

PHOTO COURTESY THOMAS BALCH LIBRARY

Belmont Manor, built 1800-1803, by Ludwell Lee

In 1781, Ludwell Lee had served as aide-de-camp to the Marquis de Lafayette, and after the Revolution he became a lawyer and a member of the Virginia General Assembly from Prince William County. He married his first cousin Flora Lee. Ludwell Lee followed his father's Federalist politics, and with the advent of Jeffersonian Republicanism at the turn of the 18th century, he retired to the realm Thomas Jefferson so admired, that of the gentleman planter. A contemporary described Ludwell Lee as perceiving "the world as a very well-ordered sphere, and though there might properly be adjustments and re-adjustments here and there, any wide deviation from the established order of things was dangerous." Another contemporary stated that when Ludwell Lee retired to Belmont at age 40, he had drawn about him "the staid and somber cloak of orthodoxy."

His manor fits this mood: heavy, but not ostentatiously so—late Georgian, architects call it. The main section connects gracefully via long passages to a pair of symmetrical dependencies. The elongated structure is not ornate or gaudy; and its front-facade brickwork, all Flemish bond—alternating stretchers and headers in each course—is considered to be the finest in Northern Virginia.

Embedded in Belmont's front wall, east of the front door, is a brick inscribed "F. L. Lee 1779," for Francis Lightfoot Lee, Ludwell's uncle and benefactor—and also a signer of the Declaration of Independence. Mr. Lee, who lived on land now Dulles Airport, represented the county in the House Of Burgesses, 1758-1769. One wonders why the brick is there.

Belmont received "The Nation's Guest" on the evening of August 9, 1825, when Ludwell Lee gave a ball for his former general, the Marquis de Lafayette, who had returned from France on a farewell visit to the United States. Lafayette, accompanied by President John Quincy Adams and former President James Monroe, then a Loudoun resident, received hundreds of people. Many walked the mile-and-a-half lane that linked Belmont and its sister plantation, Coton (now Lansdowne or the Xerox property). Slaves holding torches lit the way. Coton was then the home of Fanny Carter Lee, widow of cousin Thomas Ludwell Lee. Ludwell Lee's father would not have approved of his son's owning slaves. Richard Henry Lee believed slavery incompatible with Christianity. He once proposed that Virginia place a high tax on the import of slaves, but the legislature voted no.

Ludwell Lee died at Belmont on March 23, 1836. His grave, marked by a much newer stone and bronze plaque, is one of three remaining markers in the stone-walled Lee-Selden graveyard northwest of the manor house.

That year Margaret Mercer purchased the property and buildings from the Lee heirs. Born in 1791 at Cedar Park, Anne Arundel County, she was the brilliant daughter of ex-Maryland Governor John Francis Mercer. After the War of 1812 she became interested in the work of the American Colonization Society, a group aimed at settling former slaves in Liberia.

Her father died in 1821, and after the family paid his debts, Margaret Mercer began freeing family slaves, then paying for their passage to Africa. As her wealth waned, she obtained funds by running a girl's school at Cedar Park, and then another school at Franklin, near Baltimore. For years she had been shocking the gentry with her outspoken statements against slavery. But no one could question her insistence on high academic standards, and her schools prospered.

Miss Mercer's move to Belmont—described by a contemporary, John Jay Janney, as a "rundown farm"—may have been prompted by Ludwell Lee, who despite being a slaveowner, had been the prime mover in organizing a Loudoun County Auxiliary of the American Colonization Society in late 1819. He and the Reverend John Mines, the Leesburg Presbyterian minister (Lee was an Episcopalian), formed a group of 20 to 25 who were active through the 1820s. Ludwell Lee was the largest slaveholder of the group, owning 44 slaves in 1820. He did not free a single one, nor of record did any of the planters in the auxiliary. A list of their names read like a who's who of Loudouners: Sydnor Bailey, Charles Ball, George Carter, William Ellzey, Richard Henry Lee, William Noland, Burr Powell, and Stephen C. Roszel.

At once Margaret Mercer converted Belmont into a school for girls, Belmont Academy. Like Miss Mercer's previous schools, the academy became known throughout the South for its rigorous coursework and strong religious and moral teachings. Belmont boarded 20 to 30 girls, but it also took non-boarding students. If they were poor, they attended free. For those students, the emphasis was on basic primary subjects and agriculture.

Sally McCarty, who boarded at Belmont Academy, wrote of the school in her 1916 reminiscences:

> The great upper chambers were converted into dormitories,
> each furnished with five double beds accommodating ten girls.
> For toilet purposes a round table in the middle of the room
> served; on this five basins were ranged around a bucket of
> water provided with a dipper. In winter we broke the ice for
> our scanty ablutions. At meals a rigid abstemiousness was

inculcated; it would have been considered the acme of bad taste to ask for a second helping of anything. In winter, butter was served in very small pieces and no girl could get more than her allowance. One Sunday after the chicken had been made to go as far as possible, my neighbor at table was served with the carcass, which had the deceptive appearance of being a liberal helping. Lifting her hands she exclaimed in boarding school French: "Oh, ma chere, ma chere!" To which I replied enviously: "I think it's more than your share."

Another snippet from Miss Sally's pen recently crossed my desk, of interest because Miss Mercer had survived an attack of smallpox.

The Vaccination at Belmont

Here comes the old doctor on his little horse.
He stalks into the house and looks very cross.
"Where are the young ladies that I am to see?
Where are the young ladies, Miss Mercer?" says he.
Down comes Mary B. . . . with a smile on her face.
But then when he pricks her, she makes a grimace.
The Dr. looks frightened and Mary looks mad.
Says he, "Oh! Miss Mary, it did not hurt bad."
Then comes little Sally, yes, sweet Sally B. . . .
Oh! Don't she look pretty, just see, Dr., see,
She holds out her arm with a very good grace,
And when it is over, goes back in her place.
And then comes Miss Baker with tears in her eyes,
"I vow he shan't prick me, he shall not," she cries,
And then Lizzie N. . . . has to go in her place,
Just see, I am sure there's no fear in her face.
She comes modestly forward and holds out her arm,
For she knows the good Dr. will do her no harm.
And in this little time Miss Maria grows wise,
"I prefer a slight prick to the small pox," she cries,
Then comes Miss Markoe with a very wry face.
She eyes the poor Dr. with very ill grace,
Then looks at Miss Mercer, as much as to say,
"Indeed, Ma'am, I can't let him prick me today,"
But, Miss Mercer's determined, so, "Mary," says she,
"Go up to the Dr., you shall obey me,"
"Come, go up directly, without more ado,

I am not to be trifled with, Mary Markoe."
The next that comes down is Miss Josephine C. . . .
 Says the Dr., "Miss Phenie, & pray how art thee."
Says Miss Phenie, "I thank thee, I'm not very well,"
 "And I don't like the looks of that lance, I can tell."
Then comes Fanny N. . . .Yes, that beautiful girl,
 With lips like the ruby, and teeth like the pearl.
She walks modestly forth, and betrays no alarm,
 Gently looses her sleeve and shows a white arm,
One after another the girls all appear,
 Till at last little Sallie Smith brings up the rear.
Says the Dr., "Good morning, I'll now my bow make,
 And call again Tuesday to see if they take."
        Written by S. McCarty at
        Belmont, Nov. 1845

Always a staunch Christian, Miss Mercer studied Hebrew "to draw more purely from the fountain head," as she put it. Then, in the late 1830s, she remarked of the neighborhood: "This most uncultivated corner of the lord's vineyard. I never saw such people. The Sabbath profaned." So she asked the Reverend George Adie, rector of Saint James' Episcopal Church, Leesburg, to conduct services in the great hall at Belmont.

Soon, she decided to build an Episcopal chapel on the plantation grounds. She asked her cousin Benjamin Henry Latrobe, noted Baltimore railway bridge and tunnel architect, to design an inexpensive chapel for neighborhood use. This he did by creating a French Gothic brick front—highlighted by an elongated doorway—and affixing it to a plain frame building and belfry. Reverend Adie became chaplain at Belmont Chapel, as it was called when it was completed, circa 1840. He served until his death in 1856.

A decade before, he had led graveside services for Margaret Mercer who had died of tuberculosis. Her small gravestone, placed in front of the chapel's west facade, was later replaced by a still-standing obelisk bearing this inscription:

Sacred to the memory of Margaret Mercer, born July 1, 1791,
died 17 September 1846. Her remains repose beneath the
Chancel of this chapel, built by her own self-denying labors.
This monument is erected by her pupils as a testimony of

Margaret Mercer's Belmont Chapel   PHOTO BY JAMES BIRCHFIELD, COURTESY LOUDOUN TIMES-MIRROR

their admiration of her elevated Christian Character and of their gratitude for her invaluable instructions.

Caspar Morris, a neighbor of Miss Mercer's at Cedar Park, wrote a eulogizing biography, *A Memoir of Miss Margaret Mercer*, in 1848. Locally, she was memorialized by mapmaker Yardley Taylor—also a leading anti-slavery voice in Loudoun—who on his 1853 map of Loudoun County, paid homage to Miss Mercer by picturing Belmont and the newly erected obelisk in the map borders. Eugenia Kephart, a teacher who had assisted Miss Mercer, ran Belmont Academy after her mentor's death. About 1856 she moved the school to the outskirts of Leesburg, to the house later known as Dodona Manor, home of General George C. Marshall.

In 1838 the post office department established the Belmont Post Office because of the many letters and packages sent to the girls at the academy. Robert L. Saunders was first postmaster, serving until 1840, and after some short-timers, he was followed by John W. Wilson, 1843-1850. Postmaster Charles E. Keene, who took over in 1855, served under the Confederate postal system until the post office was discontinued in 1866.

Morris Wampler, the only male to attend Belmont Academy, figured prominently at the Second Battle of Manassas. He was the son of widow Ann L. Wampler, who also had assisted Miss Mercer at Belmont. The widow married nearby Goose Creek mill owner William Mavin the year of Margaret Mercer's death. Morris was a talented sketcher and observer of the landscape, and he made a map of the roads leading from Leesburg to Washington. He had graduated from West Point (the leading American engineering school at the time) and was trained as a "topographical engineer," the 19th-century term for a cartographer. When General Pierre Gustave Toutant Beauregard saw the Loudoun-area map, he appointed Wampler chief engineer of his command. Captain Wampler was killed in a gunnery accident at Charleston, South Carolina, late in the war.

With the teachers Eugenia and Ann gone, Belmont Manor, vacant for long stretches, fell into decay. From 1886 to 1894 it was leased by the Richmond & Danville Railroad, serving as a historic site and family outing and picnic grounds. The excursionists who came added a new chapter to Belmont's life: Belmont Park

Belmont Park
Bootleggers In The Woods

Following the Civil War, with the Belmont Post Office closed and Belmont mansion tenanted out, the pikeside neighborhood languished, kept barely viable by Jim Horsman's blacksmith shop at the site of the old post office, and a public school by the pike and Church Lane leading to Belmont Chapel and its occasional services. By the turn of the 20th century, the one-room school had closed, and so had Mr. Horsman's shop, its ruins visible till the end of the 1920s. Of the chapel, J. Harry Shannon, writer of the *Washington Star*'s "Rambler" column, came upon the site in 1918 and noted:

> Services are no longer held at Belmont Chapel and it is only at sadly distant intervals of time that a human being will pass that way, and then that man or woman will enter a tangle of periwinkle that has woven a deep green mat over the cemetery and lay a little bunch of flowers on a grave.

The grave would not have been that of Margaret Mercer, former owner of Belmont, for her remains were removed from the graveyard in 1854 and were reinterred in Philadelphia, with those of her father, who died there in 1821. Nancy Ferguson Rogers, who had lived at Belmont, recalled that the chapel was occasionally used, sometimes for marriages, and remembered a service held there in 1936.

By the late 1800s the focus of the neighborhood had shifted to the railroad. The tracks had been laid by the southern perimeter of the Belmont property in 1859. Then, the railroad was the Alexandria, Loudoun and Hampshire. Since before the Civil War there had been a quarry by Goose Creek, and now the railroad ran by the quarry, with the stop aptly called Trap Rock. The stone by that name was a fine-grained, dark-colored granite. The laborers, often former slaves, lived in shanties by the pits.

A half-mile east of Trap Rock was a second whistle-stop known as Belmont Park, a center of activity for white people. In an attempt to attract passengers, the Richmond and Danville Railroad, one of the A L & H's many successors, leased Belmont mansion from 1886 to 1894, conducted tours through the house and its grounds, and encouraged picnickers to bask on the lawns. From the station, the R & D provided free buggy service for the one-and=a-half-mile ride to the mansion. The Depression of 1893 closed this era.

The station was an open lean-to, marked by the sign "Belmont." It remained a railroad stop until passenger service ended in 1951, and the station fell imperceptibly into the underbrush. It stood just north of the tracks and on the west side of Belmont Ridge Road. On the other side of the tracks there was a well; and before the road was electrified in 1912, steam engines would rest by it while their bellies were refilled with its water.

North of the station was a store, in business from perhaps the early 1890s, when it served the excursionists to Belmont mansion. When he wasn't laying stone, G. Walter Stunkle ran the store early in the 20th century, with the business being taken over by Millard Atwell after 1906. Millard Atwell may have built the house attached to the store; both were frame structures and the store had the characteristic porch facing the road. Millard's son, Charles Franklin Atwell, took over the store in the early teens, and he and his brother, Eugene, ran it under the trade name "Atwell Brothers" until Eugene died in the 1919 flu epidemic. C. Franklin Atwell, as he was called, continued the mercantile business until 1923, and in May of that year, newspaper ads noted that Thomas Lynn of Leesburg purchased Atwell's enterprise. "He will be glad to see his friends at the store," the text read, and so he was, until the store became an early Depression casualty, closing about 1930.

South of the tracks, and still standing west of Belmont Ridge Road, was the Belmont School, successor to the old school by Church Lane. The year of its building is uncertain; the year of its closing was 1914. Louis Rollison remodeled the school into a home about 1920. On a day when he and his father, Charles Rollison, the last boatman to pole the ferry at White's, were gathering stone at Trap Rock Quarry, Charles was killed in a fall. Louis, drafted at age 37 into World War II, received a Purple Heart.

John Scott Ferguson, a Pittsburgh lawyer, began Belmont plantation's renaissance in 1907. His wife, the former Nancy Amanda Graham, was not well, and the Smoky City had been taking its toll on her health. For $30,000—one-half of it cash—she bought Belmont that October. A Pittsburgh architect added a wing and remodeled the interior. Outbuildings were added, too. Mr. Stunkle laid the stonework, including the stonewall enclosing the Lee-Selden graveyard, and the stone gates and wall that still frame the entrance. When Route 7 was widened in 1951, the stone gates and wall were moved back from the road to their present location.

Nancy Ferguson's health did improve, but her husband died, and in April 1915, she sold the 1,013-acre property, described simply, without even using the name Belmont, as "on the south side of the Leesburg and Washington Turnpike." The price was $85,000, but her daughter, Nancy Rogers, reminded me that she had spent more than that amount on improvements to the property.

Edward B. McLean was the buyer, and as was the custom among the very rich (his father, John McLean, owned the *Washington Post*), he celebrated the purchase by inviting the neighbors in for a feast. Entire beefs were roasted in open pits dug into the plantation's front field. Mr. McLean had asked Mr. Stunkle to tend the whiskey barrel, but Walter, liking his bourbon and knowing that to bartend meant to stay sober, said that drinking was against his religion. The United States Capitol was then being remodeled, and Mr. McLean bought the old stone steps leading from the plaza to the rotunda and had them moved to Belmont on eight flatcars. Any of the steps that broke in transit, exited at Ashburn station, and were used as steps to the men's room there and for Charlie Arundell's home.

But despite such goings-on, Mr. McLean could never quite match the aura of his wife, Evalyn Walsh McLean; she owned the Hope diamond.

President Warren G. Harding, a friend of the McLeans, often visited Belmont, his two-car motorcade driving up the Leesburg Pike, with his secret servicemen dutifully paying Annie Downs, and later her daughter Tillie Downs, the 25 cents due at the Mahala Tollgate at Ashburn Junction. The President's recent biographer notes that Mrs. McLean would arrange trysts for the President at Belmont, hence his many sojourns to Loudoun. After the President's death, "The Duchess," as President Harding called his wife, burned as much of his correspondence as she could to protect his reputation.

The McLeans raised thoroughbred racing horses and show horses at Belmont; and for many years their earnings from victories topped the circuit. Some 20 to 50 people worked on the farm, with Stanley True Greene managing the show-horse operation, and "Fats" Gochnauer the harness shop, which turned out all the saddles, bridles, harnesses, and leather-work. In his spare time, Fats made belts and watch fobs for the help_and their children.

The McLeans did not use the back woodland, nearly half of the property. And so, Morris Poole and Ed Ball set up a still in the back-end woods, and hired a Mr. C. to guard the still with a .25-caliber pistol. Leesburg's IRS agent, Jay Lambert, heard about the still and set out to bust the operation.

A crap game was going on amidst the mash barrels arranged in a circle in the middle of a briar patch. "Wouldn't Lambert like to see this?" Mr. C. said. Now, Lambert couldn't hit the side of a barn, and as was his custom, he burst onto the scene firing his pistol into the air. Mr. C. killed him with one shot, did some time, and lived a thereafter honorable life, raising a fine family. Locals said Mr. C. paid for doing what he had to do, for nobody else had his guts. The year was 1923.

Henry M. Horsman, son of blacksmith Jim Horsman, cried when he heard of Jay's death, and then told how Jay had saved his life.

Henry occasionally went on a drunk, and when he was in his cups, he had beaten up two of the black laborers who worked at Trap Rock. He had whipped them on his turf, but now he threatened to go into the Trap Rock shantytown. His friends then overpowered Henry and locked him up in the blacksmith shop at the Jim Maddox farm on Hay Road. But Henry found a hammer and knocked the door down. Jay Lambert had been called to the scene and found Henry staggering along the railroad track toward Trap Rock. Jay convinced Henry that he had some business to take care of in Ashburn, and while they talked, Jay plied Henry with more liquor. Henry finally passed out and awoke the next day, under a wagon in Will Hay's livery stable.

The Depression caught up with the McLeans in 1931, and they were forced to sell 75 thoroughbreds at bargain prices—and Belmont plantation for $75,000 at auction. Next year, General and Mrs. Patrick J. Hurley bought Belmont and surprised everyone by sending their daughters to Leesburg High School. General Hurley was Secretary of War in President Herbert Hoover's Cabinet.

Belmont had calmed down, with the next happening of note

coming in 1967, when a squatter who had used the decaying Belmont Chapel (described as "in shameful condition" a decade before) for a home, accidentally burned it down. For a few years the Gothic stone front façade remained upright, remindful of a scene from *Tintern Abbey*. But by 1973 it too, had fallen, and lay in shambles among the many headstones.

When IBM bought the plantation 30-odd years ago, it promised to conserve the mansion and 50 acres surrounding it in perpetuity. Recently, Toll Brothers purchased the estate to develop a residential and golf community. The company has renovated the manor house and made it the centerpiece of Belmont Country Club.

The Episcopal Church owns the Belmont Chapel grounds and graveyard, and someday, perhaps, a replica of the old chapel will arise. On Easter Sunday 1989, a small gathering from the fledgling Saint David's congregation, Ashburn, celebrated an Easter sunrise service at the damp and unkempt churchyard. If Nancy Rogers was correct in her memory, it was the first worship service at the chapel in 53 years.

Today the scene is a pristine one, for the rubble has been removed and the graveyard manicured—part of the campus of Saint David's Episcopal Church.

Ryan

**Formerly
Farmwell Or
The Five Forks**

Five Forks, or Five Corners, the village was called; but in the mid 19th century the community was known as Farmwell, the name of George Lee's vast plantation. On March 19, 1849, he and his wife Sally M. Lee gave four and a quarter acres for a Methodist Church and school at the five forks. It was the Lees' desire to "aid in the religious, moral and intellectual improvement of the people residing in the vicinity."

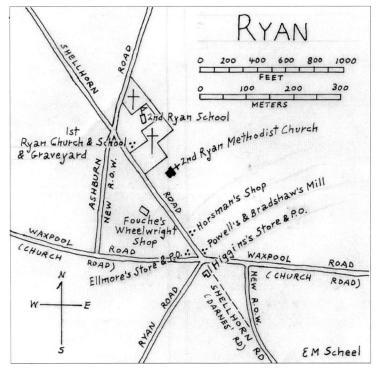

They deeded the land to five trustees residing within seven miles of the "church and school house," and the church was to be Methodist and for other Christian denominations. Within two years a graveyard was to be established for white people and a "schoolhouse for the education of all the children of white parents residing within three miles of said schoolhouse without regard to the religion persuasion of said children or of their parents." The trustees were Philip Houser, George Shryock, Richard Mann, Joseph Arundell, and William Fulton. The deed is the oldest on record for a public school in Loudoun County, and by 1853 a combined church and school stood at the site.

In 1860 the Loudoun, Alexandria, and Hampshire Railroad bypassed the five corners, and a post office named Farmwell was established at the railroad stop at present Ashburn. The five corners then became known as Old Farmwell.

The first store was built in the mid-1880s for Fran Ellmore, a crippled man, by his father to set his son up in business. In 1889 a post office named Ryan was established at the store, with Dennis Higgins postmaster. The new name, which fell in line with the post office department's policy of coining brief, easy-to-spell names, was that of John F. Ryan, who in 1883 had been elected to the Virginia House of Delegates. Mr. Ryan was also one of the area's most prominent landowners, and he served in the House until 1904. From 1894 to 1904 he was Speaker of the House, and he was also a trustee of Virginia Polytechnic Institute.

But it was the Ryan Band that brought the village its fame. Sidney Fouche (pronounced *fowsh*), who ran a Leesburg wheelwright shop, organized the band in the summer of 1895, and on July 2, 1896, the 15-member band was among more than 20 in the state to travel to Richmond for the unveiling of the monument to Confederate President Jefferson Davis. Furthermore, the Ryan Band was chosen from all of the bands present to serenade Mrs. Davis.

The band had practiced marching and playing at night. In 1961, John W. Fouche recalled that "people all along the three or four miles of their route would raise their windows and listen to the music until the last vestige of tootling and thumping had died away in the distance. [We were] like the Pied Piper of Hamelin; [children] always came trooping along to bring up the rear of the procession." Before entraining for Richmond the band had a fling at marching on Pennsylvania Avenue.

On the Richmond train, and also bound for the Davis celebration, was a group of Confederate war veterans who, when they saw the blue coats of the Ryan Band, called out, taunting: "What have you got those damned old blue coats on for?" Later the old rebs made friends with the boys from Ryan and asked them to play an old Civil War song that went: "I'm going back to Dixie where the orange blossoms grow."

The boys did not have the music for the song and did not even know the melody, but when someone began to hum it, first one, then another instrument came in, improvising so that the old soldiers were satisfied after all.

The band's arranger and leader was John Hansen, a Washingtonian, and he now knew the one song that was Mrs. Davis's favorite, "I'm Going Back to Dixie Where the Orange Blossoms Grow." It was in a lower key than the present "Dixie," so Mr. Hansen wrote a special arrangement of the piece during lunchtime before the parade.

That afternoon the Ryan Band marched past Mrs. Davis in their blue coats—the ladies whispered that they should have been gray—and gray trousers with gold braid. Dr. Charles Russell, a Herndon physician, was drum major. And when Mrs. Davis said, "Give us 'Going Back to Dixie,'" the Ryan Band did just that. They got a big write-up in the *Richmond Dispatch*.

The band bought its music from Sears and Roebuck, and on one occasion it played at a Republican rally in Falls Church for $3 a day per man—"plumber's wages" in those days. When they performed at night, they wore hats, setting up oil lamps in front. Fred Saunders once put gasoline in his. No word of what happened to Fred's eyebrows.

Their best-remembered numbers were "Liberty Bell," "Bonnie Blue Flag," "Long Shot," "Manhattan Beach," "Laddie Boy," "Home Sweet Home," and "In the Sweet By and By."

George Fouche, Sidney's brother had three sons who played—Clarence, the drum; Frank, the cornet; and John W., the trombone. George Oden Powell also played the drums, and Clarence Conrad LeFevre the big bass drum. They hired a small boy to carry it in front, and as it went past, all you could see of the lad was a pair of feet moving. Jeff Davis Lambert played the cornet, and the other members were Wallace Paxson, Fred Saunders, George Fouche, Jake Sweatbird, Will Alexander, who played trombone, Jim and Louellen Alexander, and Carl and Henry Power. Sidney Fouche, the organizer, didn't play; he just followed the band on foot. When the Spanish-American War broke out in 1898, Mr. Paxson and Mr. Sweatbird got ambitious, enlisted, and left the band to join Teddy and his Rough Riders.

The band practiced in the still-standing board-and-batten wheelwright and tin shop of George Fouche and his sons. The Fouches also made stoves, and John, in the teens, dug some of the deepest wells in eastern Loudoun. By 1920 the Fouches had gone their separate ways, and the shop was closed. John, the band's last survivor, died in 1969 at age 95.

And of the band? It broke up less than 10 years after it achieved fame. Someone in Herndon "talked them out of their instruments."

Across the street from the Fouches' shop, George Oden Powell and George W. Bradshaw operated a steam-powered flour and grain mill. The building had been a creamery in the 1880s and had been converted into a mill in the early '90s. About 1905 a one-cylinder Geyser gasoline engine replaced the mill's steam power, and a few years later the manufactory stopped grinding flour. It closed in the late 1930s and burned in 1959.

At the mill, George Bradshaw repaired shoes, and the

Ryan Crossroads, with all five corners.

magistrate's court held sway. The machinery always shut down for the justice of the peace's dispensing of wisdom, and the whole village came in to watch.

Right beside the mill was George Horsman's blacksmith shop. Mr. Horsman, who mainly farmed, generally wasn't there; and from the early 1890s until about 1910, J. B. Hurst, James W. Hawes, a Mr. Thornberry, and Vernon Cockerill, who later became the Herndon smith, ran the shop. Jim Horsman (only a kissing cousin) took over the shop about 1905 and ran it into the late 1920s.

Mr. Ellmore's store and post office passed to Jefferson D. Lambert, who in 1893 became postmaster following the one-year stint of James W. Alexander. Ed Myers ran the store from 1912 to 1916, and Charles W. Hurst, J. B.'s brother, became postmaster in 1914.

There was also a second Ellmore's Store, built across the road from the first by Dennis Higgins sometime in the 1890s. John S. Lyons ran it late in the decade, and so did Will Myers. Charles Hurst ran it from the early 1900s until 1916. It was then reopened in 1917 under George Oden Powell and his wife, Maud May. She became postmistress next year and in the '20s was village milliner. Mrs. Powell ran the post until 1930, when the second store closed, and Marvin W. Shryock became last Ryan postmaster. The mails stopped in 1946.

Mr. Shryock's post office was at the first Ellmore's Store. In 1932, Warren D. Middleton, and in 1940, Will Croson, were storekeepers. A succession of owners came after 1946, when the post closed, with George Redmon and son Franklin the only operators to run the store for a significant length of time. They were there from the mid-1950s until it closed about 1962.

Ryan had its cast of characters, but none more colorful than "Hot Ziggety." John Gordon was his real name, but whenever he got excited he exclaimed, "Hot Ziggety!" Every Christmas he set off his traditional bomb between the two Ellmore stores. He had learned how to make the mix of black powder and burlap bags during his stint in the Confederate Army. Now the whole village came to see the big flash. During his last years, in the early 1900s, Hot Ziggety made canes from sassafras and locust; he used roots to form the handles.

One business of note outside of the village was Henry Clay Harding's store, a half-mile out on the south side of the road to Waxpool. Clay, a carpenter and well-driller of note, ran the establishment in the 1890s before he moved to Ashburn. His specialty was watered-down whiskey, and in winter you brought your ice tongs for he cut the brew up in chunks. It was said "everything Clay touched turned to money."

The old Ryan school and church went separate ways in 1877, when John Shryock, the area's master carpenter, built a new church, and some 15 years later a new school. Mr. Shryock also built the 1898 Mount

Hope Church. Four years later he died at age 49 when he was building a barn in Maryland. The present Ryan church, smaller than the old one, was built in 1953.

One crow's mile northeast of town was a second church, also Methodist, built for the black population in 1891. Its land had been donated by George Monroe, and it was rebuilt in 1923. Locally, white people called the building Cedar Lane Church, for the old Ox Road on which it stood was known as Cedar Lane. Before the road was widened, one could see rows of cedars along its sides. A stalwart in Monroe's Church—as the blacks called it—was Sims Ewell, who lived nearby and made boots and shoes. His wife took in washing for all the white people.

The Ryan School built by John Shryock contained two rooms, but by 1920 only one was in use. During recess, children used to play among old gravestones and grave depressions that surrounded the building. Mrs. R. C. Mann taught there in the teens and early '20s, and other remembered teachers of that era were Tillie Monroe, Helen Van Fossen, Mary Frame, Helen Moffett, Margaret Ballenger, Lillian Ball, Mary Brady (mother of former Leesburg Mayor Kenneth Rollins), and Emma Carr, who closed its doors in the spring of 1934.

Shortly thereafter the state stopped maintaining the lower stretches of the fifth road to Five Corners, a road then called Darnes Road because it forded Broad Run, three miles out of Ryan where John Darnes had his farm. But back in the 19th century, before the road was called Darnes, Thomas Powell lived there and the road was known as Frying Pan Road. Good Baptists traveled to Frying Pan Meeting in Fairfax County by the route. You could still make it across the ford in the late 1950s, but no more.

Dr. James Towner Jones was the late-19th-century physician, but about 1902 he moved his practice to Ashburn, and later to Herndon. He was evidently not an equestrian and is remembered for his unique way of mounting a horse. He tied the horse to a tree, and then dropped down into the saddle from a branch.

William A. Quick was the other doctor, a self-taught type who never went to medical school. He was also a self-taught undertaker; appropriate co-professions. He borrowed his team of horses from Ben Harris and the hearse from Harry Sager, the undertaker in Herndon.

Dr. Quick and Harry were friends because they were both Republicans, then a rare breed in lower Loudoun. Justice of the Peace Charlie Zoll was also politically motivated, and when the United States entered World War I, he ran an ad in the *Loudoun Times* offering a monetary reward for the capture of Kaiser Bill.

"Did you get results?" someone asked him. "No," he answered, "but I made the mistake of not offering two pounds of sugar as the reward. If I had done that Tom Edwards would have got that man." Tom was Loudoun sheriff, 1906-1924, and also pharmacist at Edwards' Drug Store in Leesburg.

The five forks are now down to four.

Ashburn

Good-Bye
Farmwell, Hello
Ashburn In 1896

In 1859 the estate of Dr. George Lee, a Leesburg physician whose slaves farmed 1,236 acres called Farmwell, granted the Alexandria, Loudoun and Hampshire Railroad a right-of-way across his plantation. By January 16, 1860, daily round-trip rail service connected a new station, called Farmwell, with Alexandria.

The land had been part of Thomas Lee's original 10,000-plus-acre holdings, granted to him by Thomas, sixth Lord Fairfax in 1719 and 1728. In 1749, Thomas Lee became governor of Virginia. When he wrote his will, he gave 4,700 acres, "the remainder of all my lands between Goose Creek or Lee's Creek and Broad Run" to his sixth son, Thomas Ludwell Lee. This land then passed to Thomas Lee's grandsons, Ludwell Lee of Belmont and Thomas Ludwell Lee of Coton. Thomas Ludwell Lee's third son, George Lee, inherited 1,236 acres, and he used the name Farmwell for the tract in his October 1802 will. He died in 1805, and his only son, always known as Dr. George Lee (1796-1858), became scion of Farmwell. In 1827, Dr. Lee married Sarah Moore Henderson, daughter of Richard H. Henderson, a Leesburg lawyer, and Orra Moore Henderson. Dr. and Mrs. Lee had 23 children, and by 1888 the Farmwell tract had been divided among the siblings.

There were probably three large homes at Farmwell, one of which was gone before even yesteryear's memories. The second, commonly known as Farmwell, at least from the 1860s, was a large rambling log house. In 1935, when owner Herman Schuh took the weatherboard siding off, he told friends he found Indian darts imbedded in the mortar and logs. As there was an important mineral spring (at the lake) north of the house, the Algonkian tribes very likely used the area as a semi-permanent village and farm site. After World War II, the Church of Jesus Christ of Latter Day Saints bought Farmwell as a work farm for indigent members, and its stone gateposts became known as the Mormon Gates. Tenanted out in its later years, the building fell victim to a flue fire in 1976.

The third Farmwell house, an unforgivable 1988 casualty "of the bulldozer," is inextricably tied up in the naming of Ashburn. The appellation first appeared in 1870 as the name of John Janney's 580-acre tract. Mr. Janney acquired this part of Farmwell, west of the present Ashburn Road, from Dr. George Lee in 1841.

The Ashburn house was lawyer Janney's summer home. In winter he lived in Leesburg. Many will recall that John Janney was president of the 1861 convention that decided Virginia should leave the Union. An opponent of secession, as was the other Loudoun delegate, John Armistead Carter, Mr. Janney handed his sword to Robert E. Lee and renounced his commission with these words:

> When the Father of his Country made his last will and testament, he gave swords to his favorite nephews with an instruction that they should never be drawn from their scabbards, except in self-defense or in defense of the rights and liberties of their Country, and that if drawn for the latter purpose, they should fall with them in their hands, rather than relinquish them.

Nevertheless, it was the Leesburg home of John Janney where General Lee stopped en route to the fateful Battle of Antietam in September 1862. They were good friends; and their friendship went back many years, to the time that John Janney almost became President of the United States.

The year was 1840, and the location was Richmond. The Whigs met for their convention to nominate Virginia's favorite son, and it was a foregone conclusion that whoever was nominated would become the next Vice President. There were two nominees, John Janney of Loudoun County and John Tyler of Charles City County. The vote was a tie. The Tidewater-dominated conventioneers chose Mr. Tyler. After the convention, John Janney revealed that, as was his custom, he had voted for Mr. Tyler. President William Henry Harrison died a month after he took office, and John Tyler became President in 1841.

Joseph Holt, U. S. postmaster, appointed Noah Downs the first Farmwell postmaster in 1860, and Mr. Downs served through Confederate rule. As Mr. Downs was a strong Confederate, the post office was discontinued in 1866. Storekeeper Joseph Arundell reopened the office next year and served until 1881.

Two miles south of the village, a log church with a school arose in 1849. It was called Farmwell Methodist Church. Although the church predated the railroad depot, the community that sprang up about the church also took the name Farmwell, but after 1860 folks began to call it Old Farmwell. In 1889 the village became Ryan. One of the older names had to go, said the post office department, because sound-alike

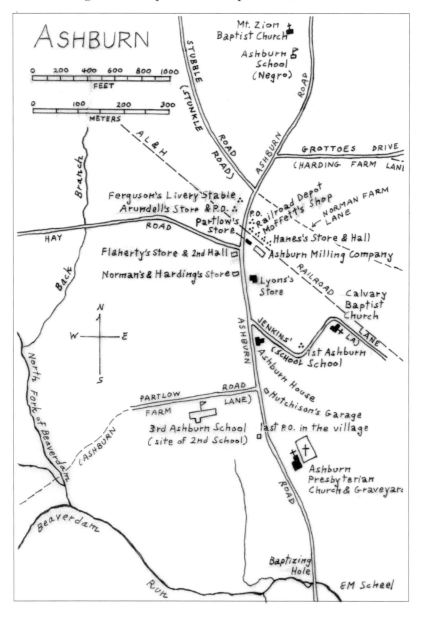

Farmville in Prince Edward County had been a post office since 1800. In 1896 it was good-bye Farmwell, hello Ashburn.

While Ashburn simply means a grove of ash trees by a *burn*, an Old English name for a spring or stream, many a resident would tell the tale of an ash tree that was struck by lightning and burned for many days. Some residents believe the "ash burn" happened shortly after Senator William Morris Stewart bought John Janney's Ashburn farm in 1895. At the time he was serving as Nevada Territory's senator, a position he held from 1862 to 1875 and from 1887 to 1905. In 1871 he declined appointment to the U. S. Supreme Court. He was known as the "Silver Senator" because he made a half-million dollars in 1856 defending claimants of the Comstock Silver Lode in Nevada and was a strong supporter of silver, rather than gold, currency. He even searched for silver in Loudoun County, probing the mine on Little Cattail and the old prospects on the banks of Goose Creek.

Sparing no expense, Senator Stewart turned Ashburn Farm into one of the state's finest dairy operations, presaging by a generation the era when one could count more than 70 dairy farms within a five-mile radius of Ashburn. Reportedly, he was the first farmer in Loudoun to pasteurize milk by steam power, and when colleagues and bigwigs came out from Washington, he would deck out his 40-man staff all in white. Mr. Stewart had the Ryan tinsmiths, John, Clarence, and Frank Fouche (pronounced *fowsh*), design a complicated rig of steam-driven fans to keep flies away from the cow stalls. Once, when he was expecting a host of senators from Washington, the house's antiquated central heating system broke down. Mr. Stewart quickly got hold of the Fouches, and in a matter of hours they had built enough stoves to heat the guests' rooms.

In the pre-Ashburn, or pre-1896, era, the village population rose to about 150. There were a bunch of businesses, starting with the stores of William O. and O. J. Orrison and their leading competitor, Moore and Fadeley, which by 1890 had become M. M. Fadeley's. The next year's Loudoun County edition of *Hardesty's Encyclopedia* notes Farmwell as "the place of residence of three ministers of the gospel, and to the credit of the citizens, no intoxicating liquors are sold within the village limits." The fourth main general merchandise store of the 1870s and 1880s was M. L. Kendrick's. It was a combined operation with his steam-powered feed mill at the site of the present mill.

The Orrisons sold out to Thomas Edward Bodmer in 1913, and he ran the store until 1940. Helping him through the years were the brothers Frank and Silas Elliott, George Bolen, Debbie Downs, and Alice Alexandra. T. E. Bodmer also had a barber shop built onto the store where Belmont's George Butler cut hair for a quarter. T. E. would give everyone in town a nickname. About 1980, the Orrisons' old store, in bad shape, came down. It had stood across the road from present Partlow's store.

Harding's (left) and Flaherty's stores, 1901

Mr. Fadeley's store, now a Weller Tile building, passed to J. E. Flaherty shortly after 1900. Then came Ernest Munday. He sold out to Lawrence and Lucius Hutchison about 1925. They went out of business in 1929, and the store was vacant for a brief time until brothers Nelson and Murrel Partlow opened their store there. Murrel returned to his Aldie store in 1935. The old Fadeley and Partlow store building was often called the Masonic Hall, for in 1905 the Ashburn Masonic Lodge organized there. Members met upstairs through 1925, and again from 1933 until 1989, when they moved to their new lodge at Ryan.

The present Partlow store, built in 1946, had been used to store feed and goods, and here Melvin and Calvin Partlow (the sons of Nelson) moved in 1950. Melvin left the business in the mid-1960s, and Calvin Partlow took over, running the store until 1985, when he began leasing it out. Today the store caters to W&OD Trail cyclists.

Shortly after 1900, Henry Clay Harding, an aggressive business-man who dealt in buggies as well as farm machinery and fertilizer, sold his concern to son Victor B. Harding and son-in-law Ernest Norman. Trading as Norman & Harding, Victor ran the business end and was the town notary. They also branched out into Sterling and Leesburg in the teens. Without heirs who wanted to carry on, they closed about 1936. Steuart Weller opened in the Norman & Harding building in 1968, and since then, Weller Tile & Mosaics has set the area standard for laying tile and marble.

M. L. Kendrick's mill passed to his son, W. A. Kendrick, in the late 1880s, and in 1903 Lawrence and Lucius Hutchison's new mill replaced it. In the late teens they sold out to William S. Jenkins, owner with entrepreneur Wallace George of Leesburg's Tuscarora Mill. With Mr. George's financ-ing, Mr. Jenkins en-larged the steam-powered mill and employed Harry Cooksey and his wife, Nettie, to run the mill. Ernest T. Harding began running the mill for Mr. Jenkins in the mid-'20s, and a few years later the

PHOTO COURTESY THOMAS BALCH LIBRARY
Harding's Mill, then Ashburn Milling

mill's power was switched from steam to electricity. Trading as E. T. Harding's Grain & Feed, Mr. Harding bought Mr. Jenkins out in 1930 and ran the mill until 1944, when William E. Fletcher took over, chang-ing the firm's name to Ashburn Milling. His son, Carlie J. Fletcher, and Roger Damewood then ran Ashburn Milling, with the operation clos-ing the last day of 1973. For about a decade the mill continued to sell feed. It is now rented as a furniture store.

Hanes's Bottom, the low-lying area just north of the old railroad and east of Ashburn Road, was the site of other businesses and of the post office, which stood by the road. From 1881, when son Charles A. Arundell followed his father, Joseph, as postmaster, until 1897, the postmastership alternated between the younger Arundell and Vanderbilt Quick. Mr. Quick had a store close to the Hanes's Bottom post office and was normally the "Republican" postmaster, meaning he usually held the office when there was a Republican president. The younger Arundell, who affixed the first Ashburn postmark in 1896, was the "Democrat" postmaster and his office was in his family's old store. John S. Ely, postmaster 1897-1914, and Mary L. Noland, postmistress, 1914-1918 and 1931-1940 had their offices at the Hanes's Bottom site. But Charlie Arundell, postmaster again, 1918-1931, switched it back to the old family store. During the early years of the 20th century, George and Elizabeth Bolen made and sold ice cream at Mr. Ely's post office, but after 1912, when the railroad was electrified, the ice cream came in by rail. The post office finally closed in 1964 and came down a few years later. Evelyn Bodmer Caylor, postmistress 1940-1969, campaigned for the move to the now-closed brick post office, last in the village.

Just east of the railroad station, in an area sometimes called "Back of the Depot" stood a blacksmith shop, run by either Stephen Heflin, "Bud" McCauley, or J. W. Hiber before 1919. All three were village smiths. Joseph E. Moffett of Herndon took over the shop in 1919 and ran it until his death in 1925.

Next to the shop, James "Old Whiskers" Moran usually parked his meat wagon and butchered beef. The Morans were numerous about Ashburn and Sterling in the three-or-so score of years after the Civil War, and their homeplace was west of Ashburn toward Murray's Ford on Goose Creek. During the war, on a hill near the homeplace, Sam Moran, then a teenager, was riding a horse, and his younger sister was holding on to him from behind. Over the rise, Sam spotted a party of Yanks. So he took off and waved his hat, and in his deep basso—later so familiar at the Ryan Methodist Church—yelled "Come on boys, we've got 'em!" The Yanks skedaddled. And that's how Jim liked to tell the story. His meat wagon and Jim Moffett's next-door blacksmith shop were gone before 1930.

George W. Hanes, for whom the bottom took its name, had his store southeast of Moffett's shop. In business from the late 1880s until the late 1920s, "Pop" Hanes did a bit of everything, including smithing and selling furniture. His "Quick Lunch," peddled to train passengers and drummers ready to ply their wares, consisted of crackers and a can of sardines. Son Noland Hanes helped operate the store when he wasn't running for the House of Delegates. His mind finally gave way. Another son, John Hanes, was the first in line for a beer license when the 18th Amendment was repealed in 1933. His beer and pool hall, open through the 1950s, had a five-gallon bucket for a restroom. In earlier years the building was a community hall and hosted medicine shows. The village literary society, named The Young Men's Lyceum, often met at Hanes's Hall. Pentecostal services were a feature of the 1920s. Standing in 1977, Hanes's is but a memory today.

South of the tracks, lumber and railroad ties—often supplied by Will Crosen and Ed Moran, and honed by George Washington Bradshaw's portable gasoline-powered mill—filled the void. G. W. Bradshaw ran two portable mills and two threshing machines.

James T. Lyons's store, still standing southeast of Weller Tile, was another leading business, in operation from the late 1880s through the early 1920s. Jim also had a store in Ryan, and was longtime justice of the peace in Ashburn. He would hold court in the store, and when it got too hot or crowded, he would shift proceedings outdoors under a large pin oak. One woman, complaining of the verdict against her, said, "You've got to hold it over; under a tree ain't no place to hold court." Jim's daughter, Mamie, who usually taught school, ran the store through the decade on the principle: If you wanted something, she'd open the store and sell it to you.

Of nearly a dozen other businesses of the 1880s through the early 1900 decades—concerns serving Ashburn's some 200 people and most of lower Loudoun west of Broad Run and north of Church Road— Green's shop was of note. Located just south of the old Flaherty store, Charles P. Green's blacksmith and coach-and wagon-making shop was in business from the late 1890s until the late teens.

North of Joseph Arundell's old store and the railroad tracks stood the livery stable built in 1913 for Lacey Ferguson, and later run by Will Hay and Will Ferguson. Hay Road takes Will's name. A horse and buggy could be rented for $2 a day—$2.50 for buggies with rubber tires. Vacationers and salesmen would tour the countryside. Will Hay always put nets on the horses to keep off the flies. Locals said the real reason for the nets was so that the renters couldn't see the horses' ribs.

The building, in poor condition, came down in the early 1980s.

Many saddles and harnesses were made by William C. Stahl, in business with J. H. Stahl from the late 1880s through the teens of the new century. His shop was on old Cedar Lane, just past old Monroe's Chapel and graveyard. It came down when the road was widened several years ago. Chester Stahl, a son, worked at Senator Stewart's Ashburn dairy farm, attended Virginia Polytechnic Institute, and became famous as the man who perfected refrigeration for dairies.

Amos Jenkins built a competing livery stable, an adjunct to his Ashburn House, a first-class country hotel, built in 1882. It was the goal of many a Washington-area angler who wanted to try the excellent bass fishing in nearby Goose Creek. The Ashburn House was also a popular stopover for those who wanted to travel the Loudoun countryside by horse and buggy. *The Loudoun Mirror* in 1909 noted rooms for 23 guests, "fitted throughout with all modern conveniences, including hot and cold baths, pool and billiard room, telephone." Charges were "$1.25 per day, $5.50 per week, or 35 cents for the single square meal."

In the teens and '20s, as weekend T-model excursions cut into the list of summer visitors, the house became a stopover for drummers (salesmen) who rented a horse and buggy, and plied their wares in the local stores and nearby emporiums of Arcola, Belmont Park, Mahala, Royville, Ryan, Watson, and Waxpool.

Catering to the T-models and EMFs ("Every Morning Fix" or "Every Mechanical Failure") was Lawrence Hutchison's garage of the mid-teens. Tom Middleton took over in the 1920s and early thirties. During that era Ed Caylor also had a tin shop in the bulding, and it was the haven of poker players and radio dances sponsored by the Modern Woodmen of America. The building then became Evelyn Caylor's house and is still in the family.

Alexander Hodgin and Benjamin Franklin Noland were the first town physicians, practicing from the late 1880s until the late 1890s. It was about 1910 when B. F. Noland's son, George, continued his father's practice. His office was in the Ashburn Hotel, where he roomed. George Noland ministered day and night through the 1918 and 1919 flu epidemics and religiously attended poor blacks living on Negro Mountain. Benjamin Franklin Noland was a pontificator, always posturing himself with his fingers in his vest and under his armpits. Even after he retired to Bassett, he would come back to Ashburn to hold audience and talk about area history. He was also a fine pianist and singer—talents that balanced his reputation as village atheist. Once, when he heard G. W. Popkins preach "Jesus Christ is free, if you accept Him." B. F. remarked loudly after the service, "Too cheap to be any good."

Physicians also sold drugs, and one day "Old Whiskers" Moran came to B. F. Noland and wanted to get some powders. He heard that if you mixed them with chicken feed, the hens laid more eggs. Dr. Noland sold him the powder for 10 cents an ounce. The mixture worked, and Jim came back for more and more. Only later did Jim find that the powder sold for 10 cents a pound at Edwards' Drug Store in Leesburg.

Ashburn residents regretted that Dr. James Towner Jones, who came to town from Ryan shortly after 1900, left for Herndon before 1918. He was temperate and taught Sunday school at both Ashburn Presbyterian and Ryan Methodist Churches. His secondhand Maxwell (often driven by son Towner) was the second-oldest remembered auto in town—next to Will Hay's one-cylinder Cadillac. Dr. Jones was careful, always asking patients the same questions over and over again. Once he took some medicine out of his bag and was ready to give it to a lady. To her surprise she saw him first take a swig. He replied that the label had come off and he wanted to make sure it was the correct medicine.

Ashburn's oldest house of worship is the board-and-batten Ashburn Presbyterian Church founded in 1876 when services were held at the old Ryan Church. The Reverend John F. Cannon, pastor of the Leesburg Presbyterian Church began to hold service periodically on Sunday afternoon in the old Belmont Chapel or school near Farmwell Station later that year. Session minutes of the Leesburg church of September 7, 1877, contain the following: Resolved:

> I. The action of the Leesburg Session in receiving certain persons as parties to be organized into a Church at Farmwell, was taken in obedience to the direction of Presbytery, and in full accord with the decision of the General Assembly.
>
> II. The Session of the Leesburg Church is directed to retain these people, not as members of the Leesburg Church, but as an association of believers to be organized into a Church at Farmwell as soon as the way is clear; and that the Pastor and Session of the Leesburg Church be requested to give all possible oversight and care to the Farmwell Congregation.

Funds were gathered in 1877 for building a church. Special "thanks [are] due Franklin Street Church of Baltimore, Central Church in Washington, and Second Church of Alexandria for contributions to the building fund," according to the Leesburg session minutes.

The land for the building, 10-plus acres, was conveyed by deed dated September 28, 1878, from the George Lee estate to James Rose, Charles Janney, and Luther Thrasher, Trustees "in consideration of the amount of Two hundred and thirty one dollars and fifty cents." By the end of 1878 the church had been completed. The area of land was "ten acres, two rods, three and six-tenths perch" as recorded in Deed Book 6 M, pages 288-289. Five acres of adjacent land were also conveyed to the Reverend L. B. Turnbull, where he later built a manse.

PHOTO COURTESY THOMAS BALCH LIBRARY

The 1878 Ashburn Presbyterian Church

Next year's report of the Leesburg Presbyterian Church notes:

At Farmwell there has been recently erected handsome church building, the largest Presbyterian Church in the county, here the congregation…generally numbers from two to three hundred people…Few [are] members of the Presbyterian Church…[many worshippers are of] a large element not specially attached to any particular denomination.

The first minister, L. B. Turnbull, served 11 years. Then, more than 22 ministers followed, laying to rest the old story that the only person to move out of a Virginia town was the Methodist minister. While many of the church's records were left on a Washington streetcar some 40 years ago, a 1909 account of the congregation's size, more than 200, notes that it had, indeed, more members than any other Presbyterian Church in Loudoun.

In 1877 the Calvary Baptist Church joined the Presbyterians, and longtime early minister Oney William "O. W." Triplett is recalled as a stalwart. The quaint frame present church dates from 1926, for an over-heated furnace burned down the first church the year before. I noted in passing Calvary Baptist recently that it had been bricked over.

Greater Zion Baptist Church, for area Negroes, has a cornerstone reading: "Z. B. Church, September 19, 1889." About 300 feet south of Zion stands Ashburn's oldest public school, the one-roomer for black children, built in 1892. It served until 1960, one of the last one-room schools to close. Periodically the old school has been for sale, and one should remember that since the recent destruction of the Powell's Grove and Rock Hill Schools for black children, this pair is the only surviving church-school duo for black youngsters in Loudoun.

PHOTO COURTESY THOMAS BALCH LIBRARY

The 1889 Greater Zion Baptist Church,

Ashburn's school for white children, a two-roomer, dated from the 1880s and stood north of the first big bend in Jenkins' or Calvary Church Lane. It closed in 1921 and was torn down in the late 1940s. Among its fine teachers were Mamie Lyons, Mary Nichols, and M. Fannie Heitoffer. Replacing it was the combined high school and elementary school, built in 1921, its cornerstone laid by members of the Ashburn Masonic Lodge. Nathaniel C. Starke, the first principal, was replaced by Richard Ely at the insistence of school board member Ernest Harding. The controversy is not to be talked about. This school, on the site of the present one, burned in 1944. High-schoolers then went to Leesburg, and the youngsters attended school at the Baptist and Presbyterian Churches, with the youngest children schooled in private homes. The next school was built in 1945 and served until the present Ashburn Elementary School arose in 1991.

The fire hall was the next modern building, constructed in 1947. The company organized at the Baptist Church, after Will Hay's barn burned in 1945. The Leesburg Fire Company suggested the idea, and Will Hay, William E. Fletcher, Richard Downs, and the Reverend Edward Hughes of Calvary were the main organizers. Dick Downs, owner of the gas station at Mahala, was the first president. With donations and pledges they bought a 1928 American Le France, which served until the 1948 GMC. The engine was garaged in another Will Hay barn until the fire hall was built.

One of the relatively new public buildings in the village was the post office, opened on Pearl Harbor Day, 1964. But it is now a pizza business, having been replaced by the post office in Beaumeade Industrial Park, built in October 1991. Evelyn Caylor had taken over the postmistress job from Mary Noland, George Noland's wife, in 1940. Mrs. Caylor, T. E. Bodmer's daughter, retired in 1969; Edna Havens, a part-Indian from Oklahoma, served until 1972. Sarah "Sally" Hertzog followed, until November 1988, and a number of short-timers have since sifted the mails for more than 22,000 suburban residents of Ashburn Farm and Ashburn Village—developments that continue to eat away at the old core's fringes.

Old Sterling   Alias
Guilford
Or Loudoun

Will Groom and others used to tell how in the summer of 1859, and maybe 1860 too, James Buchanan, the 15th U. S. President, would come out on the old Alexandria, Loudoun and Hampshire Railroad— just completed into Loudoun County—and spend some summer weekends at the old Summers place. Will would have known, for he was Sterling station agent from 1891 into the 1920s. Some folks corrected Will and said the President just came out a couple of times to see how the railroad was progressing.

After the Civil War, the house where the President stopped or stayed became a hotel and by the 1890s it was called the Sterling Hotel and was run by the Summers family. But bigger resorts out west in Hamilton and Bluemont did in the hotel. By the early 1900s it was a boarding house, operated by Mattie Summers and her niece Laura. They were open into the 1920s. The building was a shop selling odds and ends in the 1960s. Vacant since then, the volunteer firemen burned it down to get some practice—about 1985, I recall.

The railroad changed names and ownership many times. Word that President Buchanan had come to Sterling may have prompted some Washington and Old Dominion Railroad official, probably general manager George C. Baggett, to name a whistle-stop, a half-mile south of the Sterling station, Buchanan.

President Buchanan was still in office when a post office was established by the old house he had visited. But perhaps locals or the railroad thought the chief executive's name too difficult to spell or pronounce, and so they, or maybe the first postmaster, Richard H. Havener, opted for Guilford Station. The spelling was a corruption of "Guildford" (roughly meaning a trading place by a ford), a city in Surrey, England. Richard Havener served as postmaster through the Civil War, but his strong Southern sentiments prompted the U. S. government to hand William T. McFarland the job in 1866. He was followed by John A. Ashton in 1869, and John M. Hanford in 1871.

A year before, the Alexandria, Loudoun and Hampshire Railroad became the Washington and Ohio; its aim was to reach the Ohio River, far west of the coalfields of Hampshire County, West Virginia, the railroad's original goal. Either the W & O, which was looking for a new image, or postmaster Hanford, who wanted to subdivide the Guilford Station area, changed the post office and station name to Loudoun, as the station was the first scheduled stop in the county. The date was June 28, 1872, and Mr. Hanford was postmaster. Later that year kin Levi Hanford took over the office. In 1878, Levi Hanford sold several seven-acre lots to John E. Hanford and his wife, Julia W. Hanford, and to James E. Warner and his wife, Hannah E. Warner. The price for each of the lots was $10, and the location was described as near Guilford Station, a name officially out of use since 1872. Through the 1880s and '90s, James E. Warner, and Samuel Hanford, who had acquired the other Hanford interests and was living in Binghamton, New York, sold one-acre lots near the station, usually for $100 a lot. To call the area

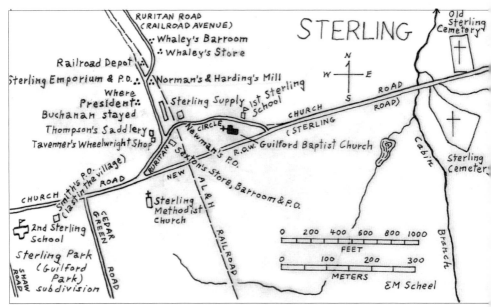

Loudoun would have been confusing, and evidently such confusion prompted the change to the name Sterling in 1887. The new name had its origin in Norman pennies of the late 11th and 12th centuries; the coins were called sterlings, and the sterling afterwards became the British pound sterling. No one recalls who chose the name for the post office, but it may have been the Hanfords or town physician, Dr. James

E. Warner, who were then carrying out their subdivision plans. Some feel the name Sterling might have been the brainstorm of one of J. Pierpont Morgan's men, for his banking interests took over the railroad in 1883, and had renamed it the Washington, Ohio and Western. Others say the name came from Sterling Farm, a 1,640-acre spread east of the village. Albert Shaw, who owned the farm, called it Sterling Farm when he bought it in 1908, but no one remembers if the name went back farther in time. Regardless, it was good-bye Loudoun and hello Sterling on March 20, 1887. Postmaster Thomas F. Sexton had the honor of changing the cancellation.

School District No. 6 was one of the earliest lot purchasers, and on October 11, 1879, it bought an acre from Mr. Warner at a discount price of $60. The road fronting the lot was called the old Church Road, a common area name in deeds of that generation. The "old church," by then no longer standing, was the pre-Revolutionary-era Sugarland Run Anglican Church that stood three miles east, astride the Loudoun-Fairfax line. The two-room school was ready for the spring term, 1880, and served until 1947, when the brick Sterling School opened.

The Methodists had built their church in 1880, on land owned by Mr. Warner and Samuel Hanford, but it was not until March 8, 1890, that the Methodists bought the property, for the standard $100, from the Messrs. Warner and Hanford. Their property, on "old church road" and "near Sterling Station," was purchased by trustees J. H. Hurst, William H. Bates, J. C. Coleman, G. W. Pool, and J. R. Ellmore. The deed was one of the first to mention the new name.

Baptists ignored the "Loudoun" designation for the community in 1880, when they purchased their lot from William F. Sexton. The Baptists called their church Guilford, and the lot of more than an acre was bought for $20 by trustees W. E. Ankers, Joseph M. Blincoe, and Nelson Potter. Their church, now vacant, was built two years later.

By the 1880s, Sterling and Ashburn were vying for the designation of capital of lower Loudoun. Ashburn would prevail because Sterling merchants could never quite match the business acumen of their Herndon counterparts, four miles to the east.

But as a summer resort, Sterling did better, and vied with Ashburn, four miles west, and Herndon Heights, two miles east, for Washington vacationers eager to flee the steamy city. An 1884 Fourth of July snippet in *The Telephone*, a Hamilton newspaper, noted the village "very popular in the second year of its new departure as a summer retreat…out of the rut of the hackneyed routine of fanciful country life." Mrs. E. G. Hanford's boarding house, which the anonymous *Telephone* writer christened "Maple Cottage," was responsible for the renaissance, and hosted at least ten guests that early summer. The writer wrote further that visitors could visit "Broad Run with touches of romantic scenery and more substantial fishing, furnish[ing] chance to expend sport, muscle and sentiment, to any one anxious to 'get up steam' with the hot weather."

Visitors also had their choice of five or six stores to shop in, and, they say, five barrooms. As you rode down the rails from Ashburn and crossed old Shaw Road, you first came across the small shanties of Negro laborers along the tracks. Many of the houses still stand, enlarged and vinyl sided. The train crossed Railroad Avenue, the dirt lane that still parallels the old railroad right-of-way, now the bicycle trail.

Sterling Emporium, circa 1900

East of the tracks stood the Whaley's store-and-barroom complex. Confederate veteran James W. Whaley had opened the general merchandise store in 1874, and for more than a quarter of a century it had vied with Thomas's barroom, Sexton's and George Johnson's stores across the tracks, and T. Ludwell Presgraves store as the largest village business. But by 1901, these businesses were no more, and Mr. Whaley now found himself in competition with his son, Carl O. Whaley, and partner Will Groom, who had taken over from Mr. Johnson. However, old Jim could still rely on that war record to bring in customers. He had served with the 35th Virginia Cavalry and had fought with distinction at Brandy Station, High Bridge, Trevilian Station, and Gettysburg. Jim Whaley had died by the time his old store closed, sometime before August 1917.

In the late '20s, Whaley's opened again under the ownership of "Uncle" Dave Beavers, who had come into quite a bit of money from a lady friend. And to the north, in an old saloon once run by Jim Whaley, Will Presgraves cut your hair for 25 cents. Both he and Dave Beavers went out of business in the Depression years of the early '30s. The old saloon and Whaley's store stood until the mid 1980s.

Across the tracks from Whaley's stood its main early-20th-century competitor, owned by the younger Whaley and Mr. Groom. In 1901, when they had taken over from George Johnson, they had a concrete-block post office built onto the store's north end. Under Mr. Johnson's reign at the store which began during the first of three tenures as postmaster, 1883-1885, the post office was right in the store. He again sorted the mails from 1889-1893 and from 1897-1907. As these years coincided with Republican presidents, we can assume the spoils system was alive and well in old Sterling. William R. Davison became postmaster, 1907-1914, and from the new block post office, Ernest Beard, Sterling's first rural mail carrier, set out in his buggy on May Day, 1907.

As "Whaley & Groom" were involved in other enterprises, they hired Henry S. Ellmore to run the store, known as the Sterling Emporium Company. Newspapers described its "almost endless variety of staple and fancy groceries" being "sold at prices that are simply startling for cheapness." But Mr. Ellmore died young, in 1915, and Will Groom had to concentrate on selling. He renamed the store Sterling Mercantile Company and ran it through 1926.

By then the store's best years had passed, for there were fewer summer boarders. Improved roads and autos beckoned them to the more alluring Blue Ridge and beyond. And Will really knew he had sold at the right time when the tolls came off the Leesburg Pike in 1928 and the road was paved. Leesburg's bigger and better emporiums were now less than a half-hour away.

Among the succession of operators who followed Mr. Groom were Otho Daniel and Herndon McGlincey, who around 1932 modernized the store. It closed about 1934, and in 1971 the Sterling fire department burned the building in a controlled-fire experiment. Nearly touching the Sterling Emporium at the south was the Summers' old Sterling Hotel, and across Railroad Avenue from the hotel was the depot. The original building had burned about 1920, but a new depot, a bit smaller, replaced it. Beside the station were cattle scales, a sawmill, and cattle pens awaiting stock to be shipped to Baltimore. The entire complex was dismantled in the early 1940s.

Just south of where old Railroad Avenue—now inexplicably named Ruritan Road—crossed the tracks, and on the west side of the rails, stood the steam-powered grist and flour mill of Victor B. Harding and his son-in-law, Ernest Norman. They called the mill Sterling Grain Company, so it wouldn't be confused with their Ashburn mill. About 1908, Edward Chick took over the Sterling mill and changed its power to a two-cylinder gasoline engine. In 1929, when electricity came to the area, the mill was electrified. Richard "Dick" Tavenner was a longtime miller under both Mr. Harding and Mr. Chick.

Mr. Chick was a fine fellow and fair miller. Once, when a young Fred Franklin Tavenner was helping his father unload wheat, Fred spilled about half a bushel—worth about $1.75, or more than a day's wage. "G. W.," Mr. Chick said to Fred's father (George Washington "Bud" Tavenner), "the boy couldn't help it; we'll give you that much wheat he spilled, and we'll clean it up."

After Mr. Chick died, his widow, Elizabeth, tried running the mill for a while. Then she married Joe Wheeler, the miller at Daleview (Brown's Chapel) in Fairfax County, and he operated the mill for Elizabeth until it closed about 1934. The building burned in 1970.

South of the old mill, where old Sterling Supply stands vacant, Whaley and Groom's fertilizer, farm machinery, and lumber business and warehouse was a fixture from 1894 into the 1920s. A 1909 testimonial for the firm noted a "leading specialty with the house is the goods of the Alexandria Fertilizer & Chemical Company, that were formerly handled in this section by Colonel [Elijah V.] White [Mr. Whaley's father's Civil War commander] and have been in use in Loudoun County for over 40 years, and every farmer that knows anything about fertilizers and farming that these goods . . . have been tested for years by the best planters."

West of the Whaley and Groom warehouse, in two buildings now connected and modernized, were Oscar Thompson's Saddlery and Flavius "Flave" Tavenner's shop. Mr. Thompson, considered by many to be the finest worker of leather in lower Loudoun, was in business from the 1880s until about 1920. Flave Tavenner partnered with B. William Presgraves and J. S. Webster in the 1890s, when their specialty was building wagons and coaches. But shortly after 1900, Flave was on his own as a wheelwright, plying the trade until about 1915.

West of Tavenner's shop stood the competing coach-and wagon-building shop of J. Samuel Ankers, in business during the 1880s and '90s. But like Flave, Sam foresaw the coming of the automobile and switched to blacksmithing in the early 1900s. In the teens, son George Ankers took over, and ran the shop until the late thirties.

Next to the complex was the favorite cutting place of Beauregard Johnston "Jackson" Keyes, the butcher. He would buy a cow from a farmer, shoot it with a rifle or hit it over the head with a hammer, skin it, and string it up. The standard price for steak was 15 cents a pound, and he would try to buy a 1,000-pounder, which he could generally get for $70. People around Sterling pronounced his name *by-u-re-gard*. He ran his portable butcher shop from before 1900 until about 1926.

Charles M. Page and Ernest Smith started up a store at Flave Tavenner's old shop in early 1930. Mr. Page had come from around Solitude, Tennessee, to work for Cecil Duff, a fellow Tennessean who had made a fortune in lumber, and who lived at Meadowbrook outside of Leesburg and owned the 1,600-acre Potomac View Farm and other Loudoun spreads. The store was called Sterling Supply, and about 1933, Charles's son, George H. Page, signed up for a Southern States Cooperative franchise that he kept until 1972. George had a warehouse across Railroad Avenue where Whaley & Groom had stood—and in 1954 moved the store to the warehouse building which he had enlarged and had outfitted with milling equipment. Sterling Supply was sold to Marion

Caylor in 1955. The business has been closed for decades, an eventual casualty of the "new" 1965 Church Road to the south of the old road, renamed Ruritan Circle in 1989.

A constant visitor to Sterling stores during Prohibition years was Earl Batt, a Southwest Virginian. He operated a large still and impromptu liquor-selling business on Ten Foot Island in the Potomac, and would buy large quantities of No. 3 brown sugar and yeast at Page's store. At Batt's Landing, still visible a 10th of a mile west of the Algonkian Park pavilion, powerboats ran whiskey from the island. Mr. Batt charged $1.50 for a false-bottom half-gallon jar.

An old-timer described Mr. Batt as "the mainstay of all of them. And he was slick. He'd have these fellows make this whiskey and he'd handle it for them. He started all these fellows—Curtis Johnson, Ralph Cochran, Clarence Jenkins—little kin, not too much. I'd get up in the morning and go down to the cows and see these stills; didn't know what they were. They had one right on a farm we rented and we didn't even know it. They moved 'em around all the time. They'd have a back way of getting into them. They didn't keep them very long in one place. They used to sell it for about $2 a pint."

As the train left Sterling and crossed the old Church Road, the still-standing but dilapidated building on the west was the successor of Thomas F. Sexton's barroom and store of the 1870s through the '90s. Here the last Loudoun postmark hit a letter on May 19, 1887, and the first Sterling postmark followed suit on the 20th. Mr Sexton's second postmastership, 1893-1897, was also in this house.

After Bill Davison's tenure as postmaster ended in 1914, Rose Newman ran the post office in a wing attached to her house, at the northeast corner of old Church Road and the railroad. Rose Newman died in 1938, and next year Mildred Kidwell Smith became postmistress, with the office still in Miss Newman's former home. In 1945, Mrs. Smith had a cinder-block post office built near the old skating rink, and it served until 1964 when a brick building at the southeast corner of Sully and old Church Road arose. After Mildred Smith retired in 1969, a string of short-timers followed. The Sterling Post Office remained at the brick building until 1976, when it moved to its present location, a mile and a half east, in Sterling Park.

At the time of its move, "Old Sterling," as the village came to be called in the late 1960s, had about 250 people, up about 100 from its heyday in the early part of the century.

The increase came about because of a subdivision called Sterling Park—not the Sterling Park you're thinking of. The original Sterling Park got its start in October 1945, when James and Nellie Ryder began selling 40 lots off their 82-acre tract between Cedar Green Road and Shaw Road. They first named their subdivision Guilford Park, and in 1945 one of the Guilford Park lots of five acres was sold to the Loudoun School Board for $1,250. A brick school, built in 1947, served until 1975, far less than half the time of the old Sterling two-roomer.

Guilford Park became Sterling Park in November, 1945, when surveyor Richard Goode platted the Ryder's subdivision. His plat was titled "Sterling Park," and thus the county recorded that name in its records. Of interest, the subdivision was the first in Loudoun County to employ restrictive covenants, the brainchild of the developer, Columbia Mortgage Company of Delaware. Each dwelling had to cost more than $2,000, and could be lived in only by persons of the "Caucasian Race." Sterling Park would follow suit in regard to race.

Daysville

Grew Out
Of Worn
Cornfields

Daysville didn't get its start until 1817, when the 20-mile-long Leesburg-to-Dranesville Turnpike, today's Route 7, was being laid through Loudoun's eastern stretches. Before that the area was just to-bacco and cornfields, worn from nearly a century of cultivation. The first east-west route, the 1740s Vestal's Gap Road, cut through a mile to the south.

During the 1820s, much of the land around today's Daysville was owned by Foushe Tebbs, and was later willed to his son, Algernon Sidney Tebbs. On January 8, 1851, Algernon and his wife, Julia, sold to George W. Miskell 110 strategic acres "on the Leesburg and George Town Turnpike…on top of the hill at a point where the new road leading from said turnpike to Scott's Landing on the river intersects said turnpike road." Those were good times, and the selling price was a heady $1,850. Today, the land is the Loudoun Campus of the Northern Virginia Community College.

Into this area, probably in the late 1830s, came Samuel Ankers, blacksmith and raiser of horses, resident of St. Mary's County, Maryland. Mr. Ankers rented pasture along various stretches of the turnpike, and noted that to get to the nearest blacksmith shop he had to go 10 miles west to Leesburg, or 4 miles east to Dranesville. So he built a small shop on the western drain of Horsepen Run, a small stream flowing under Route 7, about 1,000 feet west of today's Triple Seven Road. Mr. Ankers' shop, the first Loudoun commercial establishment on the pike east of Broad Run, straddled Horsepen just south of the turnpike. He stayed in business until the outbreak of the Civil War. Blacksmith shops were often built over a small stream so the smith could drop unwanted hot metal through a hole in the floor into the water. A prime, still-standing example is Howard Staples' shop, straddling Tanyard Branch on the east end of Upperville.

The Horsepen mentioned above, incidentally, is not the broader Horsepen Run that flows through Dulles Airport. Both names were given for horse pastures that the runs flowed through. The pens were moved from place to place. The wider Horsepen was given its name more than a century before Mr. Ankers arrived.

In 1847, with money saved from smithing and breeding, Sam Ankers struck an agreement with George Miskell and bargained to buy—probably on a lease-purchase arrangement—the 110 acres Mr. Miskell had bought from Algernon and Julia Tebbs in 1851. On Christmas Day 1856 the deed from Mr. Miskell to Mr. Ankers was signed; no selling price mentioned. Shortly after, Mr. Ankers built his first homestead, a two-and-one-half-story frame farmhouse with two brick end chimneys and gable roof, a near-twin to the Johnson Palmer homestead of similar vintage, which stood until about 15 years ago just west of the Loudoun campus.

On March 31, 1863, at the no-longer-standing Henry Green place, one mile west of the present Loudoun campus on the pike, Dick Moran, one of Confederate Colonel John Singleton Mosby's men, stopped overnight to visit Mr. Green, an old acquaintance. At sunrise next morning, Union Captain Henry C. Flint and 150 men of the First Vermont Cavalry stopped at Mr. Green's to ask directions. Soldier Moran hid until the Federals had passed and then cut across country two miles northwest to John Miskel's farm, the camping ground of Mosby's Rangers.

James J. Williamson, who rode with Colonel Mosby, described the sunrise scenario in his 1896 book *Mosby's Rangers*: A picket woke Colonel Mosby to tell him that the Federal camps on the opposite side of the Potomac River were making signals. Mosby went out into the yard to look at them when he spied Dick Moran riding toward him at breakneck speed, waving his hat, and shouting, "Mount your horses! The Yankees are coming!"

Responding quickly and with superior firepower, Mosby routed the Vermonters, driving them past the Green place and back into Fairfax County. By the time the fleeing Federals—"pursued by the Rangers who fiercely hung upon their rear"—reached the Ankers' homestead, more than three miles east from John Miskel's farm, they needed to set up a field hospital to take care of their wounded. Colonel Mosby noted in an April 1 letter to J. E. B. Stuart: "The enemy sent up a flag of truce for their dead and wounded, they established a hospital on the ground." Interred in a graveyard just west of the homestead were 10 dead, including Captain Flint, killed at Miskel's. And, noted the official Federal dispatch, "mortally wounded (will probably die today)" was a Lieutenant Grout. But Lieutenant Josiah Grout Jr. surprised them all when he left the army on a medical discharge in October. He lived on to become a member of the Vermont Legislature from 1872 to 1896, and governor of Vermont from 1896 to 1898, after being elected by the largest Republican turnout in the state's history. Governor Grout lived to be 84. He died in 1925.

Mary Fleming Ankers remembers her father-in-law, Samuel Ankers, recalling that late in the war a Confederate officer and his men passed by the Ankers' place one morning when Sam was about to feed his hogs. The officer, silent for a moment, rasped: "You just can't feed that corn to the hogs, my boys are too hungry." And the officer commandeered the corn.

In 1869, four years of peace behind, Johnson S. Palmer built a one-story frame store just west of his dwelling to accommodate a new post office. It was given the name Daysville in honor of two beloved physicians from Dranesville, John T. and William Benjamin Day. There were four Day brothers. They all were medical doctors from Calvert County, Maryland, where the first American Day on record, Robert, died in 1698. The *Washington Star* "Rambler" (history buff J. Harry Shannon) eulogized the Days on July 28, 1918:

> Best-known and best loved physicians in the country adjacent
> to Washington, Dr. William Day's practice lay east of
> Dranesville as far as Langley, Chain Bridge, Lewinsville,
> Tyson's Crossroads, while Dr. John T. Day ministered to
> aching humanity throughout the country west and south of
> Dranesville, Virginia He was especially well-known in
> Leesburg and Herndon.

As Virginians during the war, John and William Day were detained by Union Colonel George D. Bayard in November 1861. His dispatch read: "I arrested six of the citizens of Dranesville who are known to be secessionists of the bitterest stamp." The Days spent nearly a year in the old Capitol Prison at First and East Capitol Streets and Maryland Avenue, and then were released in a prisoner exchange. On September 10, 1862, they signed on as contract physicians to General Howell Cobb's Georgia Legion, serving at Antietam and Second Bull Run. Miss Leah Palmer was Daysville's first postmistress, approved by President Ulysses S. Grant in 1869. But in less than a year, as the Days' war record became known, amidst lingering carpetbag sentiment in

Washington, the post office name was changed from Daysville to Palmersville. Post offices often took the name of their master or mistress.

President Grant, however, wasn't about to lose Loudoun County votes during the next election, and within two days, on August 11, 1869, the name was back to Daysville and there was a new postmistress, Leah's mother, Anna. The Daysville Post Office was actually a continuation of the Broad Run Post Office, which closed the same day the name Palmersville was coined. The post office was moved because at the time there was no road from Broad Run to Guilford Station (now Sterling) on the Alexandria, Loudoun and Hampshire Railroad. There was, however, a road from Daysville, and so it became a natural dropping-off place for mail and goods.

About the time of the centennial, Samuel Ankers' son Arthur built a second blacksmith shop at the northwest corner of Scott's Road (now Potomac View Road) and the turnpike. It wasn't really a commercial establishment, since it served the Ankers' horses and machinery, but it was open to neighbors when in need. It operated until the early years of the 20th century and was taken down in 1921. Across the pike from the shop, the second Daysville general store was built, probably in 1881 when John W. Dailey took the postmastership away from the Palmer family and needed a place to set up shop. Daileys continued to operate the post office until it was returned to the Palmers in 1890. Then in 1895, it switched back to the newer store, this time with Beverly T. Havener postmistress and storekeeper. Daysville's last post office returned to the Palmer family store in 1897, with Richard H. Palmer, Johnson Palmer's son, as the postmaster. With the advent of Rural Free Delivery in 1907, the mails were handled at Sterling.

Palmer's store had competition from Havener's until 1902, when Sam Holsinger, its last storekeeper, closed Havener's. Palmer's store closed in 1915, and it stood abandoned, its second story removed, until 1968, when a strong wind blew it over. The store never made much money, recalls Mary Fleming Ankers, because in giving away ice cream and candy, Mr. Palmer let the children eat up the profits.

Year 1889 was a big one for Daysville, for it saw the building of the village's first church and school. A Methodist Church was organized on January 18, 1889, and services were held at the one-room Broad Run School. In October work began on the first church building, just opposite a road that became known as Greenwood Church Road, later Triple Seven Road. The one-acre lot was sold to the church by the Scott and John Miskel families for a dollar.

On October 11, 1889, church member James McClay mortgaged his farm to buy a $725 Paxton Portable Steam Engine and "Heavy Post" Circular Saw from the Geiser Manufacturing Company of Waynesboro, Pennsylvania. And W. O. Tackett, the first minister, swung the ax that felled the first tree to go into the mill.

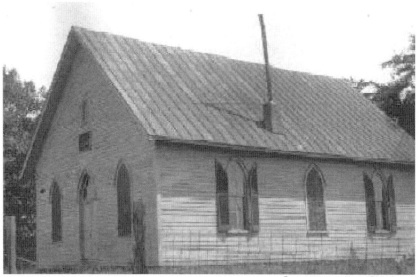

PHOTO COURTESY OF THOMAS BALCH LIBRARY

Greenwood Church, Daysville

The heavy timber came from Henry Palmer's woodlot. After the church was finished, the congregation named it Greenwood to honor its eldest member, Henry Green, whose home place was just a quarter-mile west of the church. Greenwood Church stood until 1952, when it was condemned by the state highway department for one of the periodic road widenings. The building was razed; its churchyard graves were removed to the Old Sterling Cemetery, and its pews to the Dranesville Methodist Church. The lumber went to Joe Fulcher, and with it he built a chicken house across the road. The highway department got that one, too, when it four-laned Route 7 in 1969.

Daysville's frame schoolhouse, easternmost of Loudoun's one-roomers, torn down by the widening of Potomac View Road a decade or so ago, was built late in 1889 on land bought by the Broad Run District school trustees from Eliza and George A. Beall. The selling price was $25, a standard fee for a one-acre school lot in those days. Mamie Lyons, only child of Ashburn storeowner James T. Lyons, taught at the school from nearly its beginning to its end in 1932. All children held her in great reverence, including Mahlon Austin Ankers, Arthur's son, and his children two decades later. Mary Fleming, Mahlon's wife-to-be, was still a teenager when she taught there in 1912. Two of the Loudoun Janneys, Carolyn and Lucy, also taught at Daysville. Lucy became the wife of William S. Peabody, an engraver at the Coast and Geodetic Survey in Washington, and after the two sisters died, he donated a library of basic books to the Daysville School in their memory.

In June 1910, the Ankers' homestead burned, set afire from sparks from a steam engine digging a new well. Arthur Ankers' two sons were in the midst of taking exams at Richmond College (now the University of Richmond), and he didn't tell them of the fire until exams were over. The O'Roarks, neighbors of the Ankerses, moved the displaced family into an unused house they owned, and there the Ankerses lived until their second home was completed later that year. The oak framework of the new house was cut from an eight-acre woodlot on the Ankers' farm and hauled to the sawmill at Wiehle. When electric service reached the house in the late 1920s, the electricians said they thought they had cut through steel. William Snider, a well-known builder of fine Washington homes, who lived across the pike, built the new house just east of the old. Snider's residential style was city-born, square, with hip roof and four symmetrical dormers, each topped with a wood gargoyle. There was the traditional wraparound porch with Doric columns on the south and east. The house was bulldozed, silently, early one July morning in 1976. By that time, it was sitting on the Northern Virginia Community College (NOVA) campus. When NOVA put up its main building, it couldn't find a use for the house, which hadn't figured into the architects' design for the campus. The college offered to give it away to anybody who wanted to move it, but there were no takers. If it stood today, it would have been the finest structure on the campus.

Daysville's third store, with combination home, arose across the pike from Palmer's, and by 1917 was going full-tilt under William and Ethel Brooks. Its specialty was Green River soda pop. The Brooks store ran until the late 1930s, and stood until about 45 years ago, when Dell

Adams, former chauffeur for Virginia Governor Westmoreland Davis, took it down to build his brick home. Daysville's last store, now gone like everything else, but once east of the Green place, was built for Mary Fitzgerald in 1922. She and her husband, Harry Havener, ran it until 1930, and folk named Campbell ran it during the late '40s and '50s.

Daysville was without a church for eight years until July 17, 1960, when the Potomac Baptist Church held its first meeting at a tenant house on Dr. Alfred E. Jackson's farm. Early in 1962 the church moved into a remodeled dairy barn. Dr. Jackson soon donated the barn and four acres to the church. Potomac Baptist's brick building with its angled stone front bearing a Calvary-size wooden cross shows the date stone 1975. Its congregation first met there on April 27 of that year. The old church is now, you guessed it, gone.

Ashburn's Charles S. Monroe, then a trustee of the Northern Virginia Community College Board, was the prime mover in getting a Northern Virginia Community College campus into Loudoun rather than into western Fairfax. At the time, in the late 1960s, Fairfax land was going for about $5,500 an acre, and Loudoun land for about $3,000. Reston and Sterling Park had put in their bids, but neither had enough room for the 98 acres the campus now occupies. Besides, the college didn't want to be identified with any particular community. And so, the first permanent college campus in Loudoun County since the Loudoun Agricultural Institute closed its doors back in the 1850s opened in the fall of 1974, specializing in horticulture, animal technology, communications, graphic arts, and parks and recreation. I was the college's first teacher, instructing some 10 students in the niceties of English, writing, and rhetoric, in the rooms of the now-destroyed Ankers' place.

Oak Grove

Towering Trees Pointing Heavenward

The sign "Oak Grove Rd" was missing when I last passed by, and only a "Rt. 824" heralded the half-mile-long lane leading to one of Loudoun County's oldest black settlements. The land used to be the best bird-hunting country in the county—or maybe it was Fairfax County; they never quite knew where the line ran.

After the Civil War, this pleached wood became the settling place for newly freed Negroes—because George W. and Cynthia Bell of Herndon had a business plan. In 1871 the white Bells bought a farm from Horace Payne, their idea being to make some fast money by selling off wooded sections in acre lots. Their price was a steep $75 per acre—comparable woodland in even the best sections of Loudoun was then going for $25 at most. But for many blacks who had never purchased land before, this was a time to learn.

After buying they had to contend with "Old Will" Summers, the Sterling-area assessor, justice of the peace, and chief of just-about-everything-else. Old Will was known to assess the ex-slaves' land, and when they couldn't pay, he put up their property—or threatened to put it up—for sale. Those living on the Fairfax side of the law had things a little better, and until 1958, when the boundary was surveyed for the first time since 1798, most of Oak Grove legally lay in Fairfax County.

Some of the earliest settlers of Oak Grove were the Berkley, Hannah, and Wormley families; and the oldest deed of record on the Loudoun side came December 5, 1874, from the white Bells to William Sheldon, formerly of Charlottesville. His $75 acre was "supposed to be in Loudoun County."

In 1868, the Reverend Robert Woodson, minister of Zion Baptist Church, Alexandria, came to Oak Grove and, to his surprise, found only one Baptist, Ellen Thompson. Throughout that summer, however, there were converts, and on October 10, 1868, they organized a church. The congregation apparently had no official name when it first met at the home of Ellen Thompson and her husband, William; and whether people called the church Oak Grove, or whether they called the community Oak Grove, is not known. Passed down through the generations, though, is this sentence: "This whole section was covered with stately oaks, whose towering tops pointed heavenward as if pointing toward the God whom these few followers had decided to worship in this place." Also passed down is word of the honor accorded Mrs. Thompson—"Mother of the Church."

In the spring of 1875 the congregation built a log cabin, and the once-monthly services now moved from the Thompsons' house to this cabin, which also served as a public schoolhouse. As might be expected, the December 5, 1874, deed to the "Colored Baptist Church" was recorded in Fairfax, from the white Bells, for the usual acre, for the usual price. The earliest known teacher in this school was Archie T. Shirley, who also served as church clerk from 1879 to 1925.

Before 1885 church pastors were the Reverend Woodson; William Smith, the only local pastor; Wilson Gordon of Alexandria; and L. H. Bailey of Occoquan. The Reverend James A. Scott of Falls Church came in 1885 and served until 1897. During his tenure, a board-and-batten church might have been built, for on September 18, 1888, additional land was purchased from Thornton and Hannah W. Wormley. In the deed for that sale, the church is called Woodson Mission Church.

In 1897, the Reverend S. M. Johnson of Alexandria became pastor, and he served until 1925. The leaders of the church in these early years, some of whom probably built the first two churches, were Washington Wormley, William Thompson, William Sheldon, Charles Berkley, Henry Tutt, Fayette Smith, Dallas Jackson, Moses Nicholas, Henry Lucas, Isaiah Plummer, Reason Williams, and Robert Baylor. During that era Ashburn's Greater Zion Church and Floris's Mount Pleasant both were born from the Oak Grove Church.

No one knows how long Jim Jackson had his store just across from Woodson Mission. Some say he began in the 1890s. Some say earlier. He was a quiet man, and his store was quiet. He didn't sell clothes, and didn't sell meat—just fatback. In later years he sold Richmond Benefit insurance door-to-door. He was an elderly man when he closed his businesses about 1932.

In the early 20th century, most in Oak Grove did their heavy shopping in Herndon or Sterling. They either walked on the rutted lane by the railroad or walked a half-mile down track to the resort community of Herndon Heights. At the Heights there was a lean-to-type station, and if the engineer saw people by the lean-to waving the flag, he stopped. The conductor charged a dime for the mile ride into Herndon or for the two-and-a-half-mile ride into Sterling. By 1918 or so, a new lean-to was put up, and below its overhang were the words "Oak Grove." The stop was just across from the church, and the fares to Herndon and Sterling were the same.

Shortly before World War I, more Oak Grovers shopped in Herndon even though Will Groom's Sterling Mercantile was said to be the biggest country store around. It's not that folks resented the days of Old Will Summers' intimidation, but the two-mile trip to Sterling sometimes took half an hour. Less than a quarter-mile up track from Oak Grove was a stop called Lynn, or Lynn Station, and there was a big milk-loading platform at the stop. Harry Lynn was the unofficial Sterling area vet. His brothers were Arthur and Wade, and his sister was Lenah.

And half a mile before you got to old Guilford Station at Sterling, there was another flag stop called Buchanan. In reality it was a loading platform for Old Will Summers' farm. According to Will, he was the one who named the stop Buchanan because it was where, as a young boy, he had met President James Buchanan, who was on his way by rail to his summer White House at Sterling. As a salute to Old Will, all trains at least slowed and blew their whistles.

Another story about the way Buchanan got its name: the railroad changed names and ownership many times. Word that President Buchanan had come to Sterling may have prompted some Washington & Old Dominion Railroad official, probably general manager George C. Baggett, to name the whistle-stop Buchanan.

Jim Jackson's was the only business Oak Grove ever had, but a half-mile away, in 1938, a Mr. Quesenberry (pronounced *kwiz-in-ber-ry* up here) built a block store and operated it for a year or two. The Norton family soon took over, and Harry Kelly bought it from Carlin Wilson in 1957. Charles H. James acquired it in 1977, and this last of the original Sterling-area stores was still going strong into the eighties. "James Gen'l Store" the sign read, if you were traveling on the old Ox Road (Route 606), but those days are over.

Times had started to change in the 1890s. Fairfax County had built its first Oak Grove School, after the board-and-batten church was built. It was a frame one-roomer. Flossie Coleman and Annie E. Calbert of Houston, Texas, taught there. During the teens, school shifted to the home of Annie Brown, and there Thelma Adams Gainey was teacher. About 1920, Fairfax County and the Julius Rosenwald Foundation built a frame two-roomer. Julia Hall, Josephine Hendricks, and Winnie Spencer were teachers, and the school served until the last of the Oak Grove schools, the brick four-roomer, was built on the Ox Road to Herndon in 1948. Ten years later, when Oak Grove was found to be located in Loudoun, Fairfax wanted to charge the Loudouners tuition. The Loudoun school board, not wanting to pay the nominal fee for 40-or-so children, bused them all to Leesburg, nearly an hour's ride away. The one-roomer stood till 1935; the two-roomer, till '75. The brick school is now the Herndon police department.

During the early years of the 20th century, a frame Odd Fellows Hall and Household of Ruth fraternal building joined the church. It closed by the late '40s though, its members having moved away or died.

Oak Grove Church, however, was growing. Its choir, begun by Pastor Edgar Newton in the late 1930s, was soon appearing in Leesburg, Calvary at Ashburn, Guilford at Sterling, and at Mount Pleasant Baptist near Aldie. The congregation had grown to about 100, and by the early 1940s the church held two services a month, on the second and fourth Sundays. In 1944, parishioners Frank Baylor and Oliver Branham, Sr., raised a new church of shingles, but fire destroyed the building on January 17, 1957.

Some congregants deserving mention during these middle years of the 20th century: Sister Katherine Plummer, who at her death in 1945 left the church her entire estate of land, home, and personal property; Sister Jannie Jackson, who left her life-insurance proceeds to the church; Mollie Newman, church clerk, 1942 -1989; Ruth E. Williams, church treasurer, 1953-1975; and sister Ada Lee, who in 1998 was "sent home to Glory at an earthly age of 107." She had been a member of Oak Grove Church since 1908.

Under the leadership of the Reverend Clinton L. Rogers, pastor from 1947-1975, a fourth church arose in 1958, and in 2000 the present brick church replaced it. The Fifth church, significantly larger than its predecessor, is a tribute to the Reverend Hennie Brown, Jr., of Wheaton, Maryland, pastor since 1976. But in traditional fashion, the church's

2001 history gives credit to another: "We have sailed the era of time from 1868, through 133 years to this present day because our Captain is Jesus Christ our Lord."

PHOTO COURTESY *COURAGE, MY SOUL*

The fourth Oak Grove Baptist church, 1958

Nokes

Honoring
Another
George Washington

The community of Nokes, sometimes called Nokes Mountain or, by old-timers, Bridges' Hill, was settled by freed slaves and blacks after the Civil War. Along with Oak Grove, Willard, and Conklin, Nokes became one of the four black neighborhoods in the eastern stretch of Loudoun County.

By the waning years of the 19th century, Bridges' Hill began to take on another name, used only by black people. That name was Nokes, honoring George Washington Nokes, ex-slave of an unknown Loudoun family. Mr. Nokes had leased land from the Blincoe family after the Civil War, but he did not save up enough money to buy land until 1901. The deed was signed on President George Washington's birthday.

Mr. Nokes and his wife, Caroline, purchased five acres on the "south side of the old Broad Run road" (formerly Thayer Road, for farmer George Washington Thayer, and today Marie's Road, for Marie Waddell) from Martha S. Blincoe for $175.

The Nokeses' son Albert and his wife, Carrie Dade, had six children: Samuel, Albert Carl, John, Forest, Clarence, and Katie. In April of 1978, when I last saw Clarence Nokes, the one surviving child, he was 88 and the dean of the neighborhood's black families.

George Washington Nokes and the area blacks who still rented land were subsistence farmers, and on their few acres they planted a large garden and a corn patch, and they kept a few hogs, a milk cow, and perhaps a heifer and steer. They lived in small cabins and weatherboard homes, unpainted for the most part. None still stand.

When these men were not working their own spreads, they worked for the white farmers in the neighborhood, and they also cut wood and fashioned it into barrel staves, railroad ties, implement handles, and other tools, shipped via the railroad at Sterling depot.

Three of George Washington Nokes's sons—Albert Carl, Samuel, and Clarence—followed their father's example and were the next buyers of land at Nokes. Albert Carl and his wife, Ada Frances, bought a frame home on 3 acres previously owned by Joseph P. Baumback on August 10, 1904, for $116 at a court-ordered auction. The couple added to their holdings on July 23, 1910, when they purchased 6.2 acres for $100 from Henry S. Smith and his wife, Maria L. Smith. On January 17, 1911, Samuel Nokes and his wife, Daisy, bought 8 acres from Thomas W. Grimes for $10 down. The full purchase price was not stated in the deed, but in October of 1912 they owed $144.25. On June 10, 1915, Clarence Nokes bought 10 acres with a frame dwelling for $650 from John Walter and his wife, Eliza. Mr. Nokes was able to afford a $400 cash payment on the property.

Fred Franklin Tavenner of Sterling told me a bit more about Clarence and Ada in 1977:

> Clarence Nokes is living there yet; he worked for me for 30 years. Might have been a little store there, fellow that bought Sam's place, but it didn't amount to much. I guess Carl was the oldest; he worked for me for a long time. I remember his father as a kid. Ada was [Carl's] wife. She was a real good old colored gal. She liked her drinks, but she really did help people. She had all kinds of ways of doing things. Like my mother, when any of us was born, they'd try to have her. Whenever anybody got sick, she'd try to help. The school belongs to Clarence; he also bought the house that belonged to Carl. Ada and Carl, they never had any children.

The community had its first schoolhouse when the Nokes clan prompted the Broad Run School District trustees to move a shanty to the area about 1917. Within five years this one-roomer school burned, but the trustees said they would build a new one if area residents would buy the land for it. By then the various Loudoun school boards were insisting on purchased plots for new schools. Previous rural schoolhouses had often been built on unused portions of farms with permission from the landowner.

Perhaps the school board realized that some of the Nokeses and other area blacks were growing prosperous—at least by local standards. Tax lists for 1920 noted that Carl and Ada Nokes's 9 acres was valued at $90, and their home at $150. Clarence Nokes's 10 acres was valued at $80, and his home at $200. Samuel Nokes's 8 acres was valued at $80, and his home at $100.

While the area's black citizens raised money to buy land for a new schoolhouse, classes were probably held in an unused, rent-free neighborhood dwelling. Families who donated $125 to buy the one acre for the new school were the Nokeses; William Edds and Austin Fitts—the most prosperous area blacks, they lived at Pigeon Hill on the present Countryside tract; the Ewings, probably Thomas and Alice J. Ewing of Sterling; and Lafayette and Henry Robinson of Willard. They gave the money to spokesman Albert Carl Nokes, who on April 30, 1926, bought property from widow Dollie Hermes's heirs and the next day deeded the one acre to the Loudoun School Board. (The various magisterial district school boards had been consolidated in 1922.) The deed noted: "land with school house thereon...now used for a colored school." Thus it appears that the Nokes, Edds, Fitts, Ewing, and Robinson families paid for the building as well as the land.

In 1929 the Nokes School closed for lack of children, but in 1942, at the request of Dr. Claude Moore, it reopened. Dr. Moore had some farm help up from Culpeper County. They were James and Jesse Fry and their several children. The school's main teacher from the 1920s through the 1940s was Cornelia Ewing; and the teacher who in 1957 closed its doors for the final time was Nannie Cole. The Nokes School burned in 1965; for two decades its blackened shell remained visible.

During the Second World War, the Reverend John Thornton and his wife, Edna, operated a small general store at Nokes. Now people didn't have to walk the two miles to Sterling to shop. They didn't want to take their cars because of gas rationing. In 1962 the Thorntons founded the area's first church, its date stone reading "First Baptist Church Organized Jan. 28, 1962. Built 1964. Founder J. W. Thornton." Locally the church is sometimes called "Johnny Thornton's Church."

To make room for commercial structures at the north and west sides of Nokes Mountain, a good third of the hill was gouged away in the 1980s and early nineties. The old Nokes places are gone. Few of the old black families remain.

Conklin

Mary and Joseph
Tended
The Store

"Old Man" Conklin, as he was called, passed on about the time of the First World War, as did the post office that took his name—nearly 200 years after this area in Loudoun's extreme southeast was settled by planters from down-river Potomac plantations. Grants in those days usually mentioned the upper drains of Elk Lick, named about 1715 for red deer that looked like elk licking and lapping along the stream's banks.

Joseph R. Conklin and his wife, Mary, settlers from Gregg Township, Union County, Pennsylvania, bought an unspecified amount (though well over 100 acres) of land, from Horace Adee in 1871. The price was $500, and the location was then known as the corner of the Catharpin-to-Gum Springs Road and the old Braddock Road. Locals did not call it the Braddock Road until about that time, for this oldest east-west road in Loudoun was generally known as the Colchester Road. It dated from the early 1740s, and went from Williams's Gap (later Snickers' Gap) in the Blue Ridge, east to the Fairfax County tobacco port of Colchester.

The name Braddock Road came about because of some strange happenings. Early in 1755, when British Major General Edward Braddock was planning his march to Fort Duquesne (now Pittsburgh), where he thought he was going to whip the French, he decided it would be best to send one of his brigades northwest by the Colchester Road. Officials of the Maryland Colony knew that the best way to widen and pack down a rutted track was to send an army over it. So with some good public relations, they persuaded the General to come through old Route 40 in Maryland, rather than through today's Braddock Road in Loudoun County. Therefore, the general never came through Loudoun, although he did send his second brigade, under Sir Peter Halkett, down what is roughly today's Route 9, and its easterly continuation, the old Vestal's Gap Road. George Washington, writing to William Fairfax on May 5, 1755, told the story:

> You will naturally conclude that to pass through Maryland
> (when no object required it), was an uncommon and extraor-
> dinary route for the General and Colonel [Thomas] Dunbar's
> regiment to this place [Winchester]. Those who promoted it

had rather that the communication should be opened that way, than through Virginia; but I believe the eyes of the General are now open, and the imposition detected; consequently the like will not happen again.

Happen again it never did, for General Braddock met his end at Fort Duquesne. He was the hero of his day, and the Braddock Road was named for him. But the road really owes it name to a rumor that gradually changed what never happened into what should have happened, and then what did happen. To boot, area historian W. H. Snowden helped the rumor along in the late 19th century by misreading John Dalrymple's notes on the Halkett march. And since Sir Peter's diary—clearly noting the three area stops: Coleman's Ordinary on Sugarland Run, Fruitlands, east of Leesburg, and at Israel Thompson's at Wheatland—was not available to Mr. Snowden, he flatly stated that Braddock came through Loudoun via the old Colchester Road and Snickersville Pike.

Back to the Conklins, who may have been in bad straits, for in 1874 they filed these words in a deed book, claiming that under provisions of the 1862 Homestead Act, their following properties be exempt from debts or liabilities:

> Three cows of the value of $50, one being red and the two remaining brindle in color, one bureau of the value of $15 and with certain tract of land situated in said County of Loudoun containing about 200 acres adjoining Mary Conklin, Horace Adee, and Hutchison's heirs of the value of $1,200. Also all my estate and interest in a tract of about 50 acres belonging to my wife adjoining the above tract of the value of $400 making a total of $1,665.

In 1872, two years after the Conklins came to Loudoun, the village-to-be's first public school arose. Its description in the 1871 deed from Horace Adee, who gave the parcel for Broad Run School District, reads "forever as a situation for a school house for colored children." The frame one-roomer on stone foundation was always known as the Conklin School.

Conklin's first store, at the southeast corner of the old Colchester Road and Ticonderoga Road, was a one-room frame building with a small porch. It was built to house the village's first post office, established in 1890 with Eugene Utterback the first postmaster. Joseph and

Mary Conklin ran the store; hence the name on the postmark. In 1892 Joseph Conklin accepted the postmaster's job. He served until 1895; then Charles R. Skillman took over until the post office closed in 1917 and the mails shifted to Arcola.

About 1910 the Conklin store burned down, and "Old Man" Skillman moved his stamps and cancelers a half-mile east to the newly built store of Eddie O'Meara at the southwest corner of the Colchester and Bull Run Post Office Roads. The latter road had been given that name because it led to the 1878 Bull Run Post Office in neighboring Fairfax County.

Conklin's second public school, for white children, was built in 1889, and was called McGraw's Ridge after the 400-foot-high ridge it stood on. The ridge was named for Richard McGraw and his family. Richard took out a 296-acre grant along the ridge in 1741, and an "Old Man" McGraw, who passed on early in the 20th century, is still recalled.

One of the remembered teachers at the German-siding one-room school was a Mr. Kidwell. Early in the 1900s he taught its 25 to 30 children in seven grades. To supple-ment his $30-a-month salary—and to keep his sanity—he raised chickens. Now Mr. Kidwell's pupils knew noth-ing of the chickens. One day, on their way home from school, a group of boys, led by young Roy Hagenbuch, spotted a rooster perched on a fence post. Roy took aim at the rooster with a rock. The youngsters had no idea that the rooster belonged to Mr. Kidwell or that Mr. Kidwell was watching them from behind his screen door. Roy's aim was good, and so was Mr. Kidwell's. Next day, Roy got his hide tanned; for the longest time, he couldn't figure out the reason.

Photo courtesy Loudoun Times-Mirror
Old Fairview Church

Fairview Methodist Episcopal Church became the Conklin area's first house of worship in 1897. Built on land donated by A. H. Lee, its German siding, high-pitched roof, and twin brick chimneys are indicative of the era's cottage style. The church was named for its fair view, looking westward across the Bull Run Valley and to the Bull Run Mountains. Fairview Church closed its doors about 1950, and in 1953, Dewey S. Allison, sole surviving trustee of the Fairview Episcopal Church South, sold the building for $500.

Conklin's second church, Prosperity, bears the date stone: "Prosperity Baptist Church, July 30, 1899." Its members were "New Schoolers" (unlike the Old School Baptists, they believed in paid ministers, Sunday school for children, missionaries, and music to accompany the choir). The church stood on land donated by Charles Dean that was part of a 142-acre tract willed to Mr. Dean by Thomas Settle in 1886, for the recipient had been a trusted slave of Mr. Settle's. Two log-cabin slave quarters, linked together and sided over, yet survive on the Settle-Dean farmstead.

Remains of the Settle-Dean Slave Quarters   <small>Photo courtesy of County of Loudoun Dept. of Planning</small>

One of Charles's three sisters was the noted black missionary and crusader Jennie Dean. She was born a slave in 1852, on land north of the Manassas battlefield, near Sudley Springs, Prince William County. Miss Jennie, as she was called, raised funds to build Prosperity, with most of the money coming from a Mrs. Wilcox of 15 Holyoke Street, Boston. Miss Jennie, a crusader for equality in education until her death in 1913, also raised funds for the Mount Calvary Church organized 1880 at Catharpin, and the Dean Divers Church organized 1900 near

Manassas, both in Prince William. She was also responsible for building that county's Negro high school, the Manassas Industrial School, in 1894. Before Douglass High School was built in Leesburg in 1941, most blacks who attended high school in lower Loudoun went to the accredited Manassas school. A few boarded at the school, but most car-pooled

Miss Jennie's 1896 pamphlet, "Jennie Dean's Rules For Good Behavior Among Her People," was a classic in its day, especially timely since the return of Democratic Party control to Virginia politics in 1890 heralded the 1902 State Convention that effectively disenfranchised blacks by imposing arbitrary "literacy tests" and a poll tax few could afford.

Eddie O'Meara emptied his store shortly after the post office closed in 1917, lamenting that there would be no place where people could hear gossip. He became a builder and enlarged and remodeled the old post office into a dwelling. And so it remained until it was taken down in 1961.

McGraw's Ridge School closed its doors in 1939, when the brick school at Arcola opened. The last teacher was Bertha Warren Royston of Middleburg, successor to Mr. Kidwell, Ed Crouch, and sisters Eva and Virginia Hunt. Three years later, McGraw's Ridge School burned to the ground.

Conklin School survived as a center of learning until 1948, when the Negro schools in lower Loudoun consolidated, and the pupils were bused to Leesburg, often an hour's journey away. The school board abandoned Conklin School in 1955, and it burned a few years ago.

Fire of unknown origin hit Prosperity Church in 1951, but next year a larger church was built a bit to the east of the first church. For 20 years the congregation worshipped in the basement, until the second story, concrete block with brick piers, arose in 1972. The block was stuccoed in 1976. A new date stone tells the story: "Foundation built-1952, Rev. S. Pearson Pastor. Church Rebuilt-1972 Rev. N. W. Smith Pastor."

It was not until 1956 that they paved the Elk Lick or Conklin Road south from Route 50 into Conklin. The road had been known as Rector's Road, as that family lived on the road's upper reaches in the 1920s. Before that it was called New Cut Road, one of several "new cuts" in the county, for it was first cut through about 1885. No sign marks the entrance to Conklin, but there's a gentle bump over a wooden bridge crossing the Elk Lick that says about as much.

The way into Conklin, not so long ago

PHOTO COURTESY THOMAS BALCH LIBRARY

Pleasant Valley

Also Known As Frizzleburg

It's pleasant, all right. Today, driving along Route 50 from Fairfax into Loudoun, you'll notice a Pleasant Valley subdivision sign at the corner of Blevins' Road. But you won't see a valley. This stretch begins the Pleasant Valley neighborhood. It took its name back in 1818, when on October 29 Elijah Hutchison opened the Pleasant Valley Post Office, its location about a half-mile east of the Fairfax-Loudoun line. The "valley" was a gentle slope down to Cub Run, named nearly a century before for an errant small bear.

Mr. Hutchison ran a store at the post, and in 1837 he gave both jobs to his son William, who in 1847 handed the reins to William H. Fitzhugh. Then came a rapid succession of postmasters— James H. Joliffe, James H. Palmer, William W. Palmer—until James H. Whaley took over late in

PHOTO COURTESY ARLEAN HILL

Once a pleasant Pleasant Valley home

1854. On January 4, 1856, James L. Cross became postmaster and store-keeper, and by that time there was a saying at Pleasant Valley that only if your first name was James or William could you handle the job.

James Cross was Confederate postmaster and that meant he was out of a job by 1865. He handed the post back to William W. Palmer, who said he was a Republican, but wasn't. So James H. Whaley came back in 1868. In 1873 he handed over the post to Ellen V. Hamilton, one of Fairfax County's first postmistresses. She worked less than a year. Burr W. Garrett became postmaster in 1874.

About this time, the post office moved west from its Fairfax County location by Cub Run, to Samuel Gillam's store straddling the Loudoun-Fairfax boundary. James W. Gaines took over the post duties from Burr Garrett on the third day of 1878. Later that year he decided that his wife needed the $300 salary—so Susan V. Gaines became postmistress. She, at least, stayed four years. In 1882 when Charles L. Hutchison became postmaster, he moved the office back to where it used to be, in Fairfax County by Cub Run, at or near Russell Rector's store of recent vintage.

The oldest Valley business within anyone's recollection is Jim Buck Poland's store at the northwest corner of the Little River Turnpike and Poland Road. It opened about 1889 and closed in 1943 or 1944. Jim Buck sold the area's first hair curlers, and they were much fancied by neighborhood young women—so much that the ladies would come by with their hair in curlers. Men sitting about the store barrels dubbed the corner Frizzleburg at the century's turn.

Another 19th-century business within memory was the blacksmith shop of Jim Sinclair, one of Mosby's Rangers. His shop, at the site of the "Nut Hut" in 1979, led the exodus of Valley businesses back to Loudoun County. Mr. Sinclair was smithing in the 1890s, and his shop closed in 1909. Joining Mr. Sinclair's shop about 1900 was Ashby Smith's steam-powered grist and sawmill at the southwest corner of the Little River Turnpike and Poland Road. The mill closed about 1920. It was in this building that Tom Middleton opened the first neighborhood garage in the 1920s.

Along with the gentlemen who established businesses, many in the neighborhood drove market wagons—huckster wagons, they were called—into western Loudoun to pick up produce and sell it in populous Alexandria or Washington. R. T. Maddox drove a wagon for many years, and sometimes he and others would drive cattle and turkeys into the city. People always remember the turkey drives, for the birds would roost in the trees at night.

Pleasant Valley's one-room school was standing on October 20, 1891, when, for one cent, L. Frank Palmer sold its quarter-acre lot to Ludwell Hutchison, John Shryock, and Walter V. Hummer, school trustees of District No. 6. Some of the remembered teachers at the school, which closed in 1918, were Eva Matthews, Mary Frame, Mary Hixson, Tillie Moore, and the one gentleman, "Preacher" Vaughn.

On August 30, 1893, Fannie Whaley and Alonzo O'Bannon donated one and an eighth acres for "a place of divine worship for the use of the ministry and membership of the Methodist Episcopal Church

South." The Pleasant Valley Church was dedicated in 1895. Trustees of the 53-member congregation—an outgrowth of Sterling Methodist— were George W. Pool, J. Thomas Presgraves, Edwin Cross, Alfred Daymond, and John Skillman. The Reverend C. E. Sutton was the first minister. The brick educational building that joins the frame church was built in 1946, and the Reverend Woodward W. Hayzlett and his wife, Jane, were the first to move into the parsonage, in June 1947.

By 1910 or so, there were two separate communities: old Pleasant Valley in Fairfax County and new Frizzleburg in Loudoun. The always-changing Pleasant Valley postmasters were George W. Mankin, who followed Charles Hutchison in 1887; then Lewis F. Palmer Jr. came on in 1890, Edward S. Hutchison in 1895, and George W. Taylor in 1905. Under Mr. Palmer and Mr. Hutchison in the 1890s, B. G. Benton, and later Frank Anderson, ran the store. George Taylor was the last store operator at the post office, and sometime during his tenure, the post office moved back to a bandbox building right on the Loudoun County line, where it had been before 1882. There it remained when George H. Hutchison became the last Pleasant Valley postmaster, an office his forebears began 98 years before.

On April 29, 1916, the post office closed, and the mail was distributed from Herndon. The first Rural Free Delivery carriers named the roads: Blevins Road, today's Route 609, for Dr. James Blevins, who lived by it and practiced dentistry in an office back of the Methodist Church. Sowers Road, today's 639, was named for farmer Phil Sowers and wife, Annie. Poland Road, Route 742, was named for Jim Buck Poland's store, with a nod to farmer Alpheus Poland.

At Frizzleburg the businesses continued. About 1916, Joe Poland opened a gasoline-powered grist and sawmill across the Little River Turnpike from Jim Buck's store. It ran four or five years. Joe Poland also opened a blacksmith shop, run by Aubrey Skillman. It operated into the mid 1920s. Joe Poland's mill was followed in the early 1930s by the gas-powered gristmill of Tom Crouch. Tom's father, John Crouch, had built many of the area's turn-of-the-century homes. There was even a doctor, Ira Thomas, who practiced in the 1920s.

Thirty to 40 schoolchildren a year were too many to handle, so in February 1917, the Broad Run School District, successors to District No. 6, bought additional acreage from Ashby and Sallie Smith. That fall, a second school, a two-roomer, was completed. Remembered teachers are Daisy and Blanche Hutchison, Ellen Collier, Creola Daniel Wilson, Zelma Roller Marshall, and Mae Poland. Robert Myers served as principal in the school's last years. New Pleasant Valley School, also remembered for its 10-foot-high Philadelphia shingling in its interior, closed in 1939, when the new Arcola School took the place of the old Arcola, Carter's, McGraw's Ridge, and Pleasant Valley Schools. Delmas Glascock then opened a store and beer parlor in the former Pleasant Valley School. Molly McAllister and others tended the establishment. Pleasant Valley School burned in the spring of 1975, but its distinctive shingling stood upright for a few years more.

Old Pleasant Valley was revived somewhat in the mid-1920s when Russell Rector's store opened. Wade and Benton Hutchison established a garage across from Rector's store in the 1930s and 1940s. In the next decade, Gilbert and Stanley Presgraves took over the business. The four-laning of Route 50 in 1974 took away Rector's store, as well as the entire north side of Pleasant Valley. Today, with just a pile of rubble that was once its school, most call downtown Pleasant Valley the slight rise and grove that shelters the venerable Methodist Church.

Lenah

Maybe Philip's
Girlfriend Was
A Lenah

Lenah got its start in 1806, when the Little River Turnpike Company built the tollhouse by the north side of a newly completed road from on the Little River at Aldie. There was no village of Lenah then. Most people, in fact, called the tollhouse and the area about it the Little River neighborhood after the nearby 1769 Little River Baptist meetinghouse. From 1831, the neighborhood was known as Arcola because less than a mile east of the tollhouse stood Matthew Lee's Arcola Post Office.

The sturdy clapboard tollhouse with its big stone chimney was a fitting tribute to Phineas Janney, director and overseer of the Little River Turnpike Company from 1817 to 1853. In between the "thee's" and "thou's" of its reports to the State Board of Public Works, one can see that it netted $10,000 to $12,000 a year while just about every other Virginia pike was going broke.

PHOTO COURTESY THOMAS BALCH LIBRARY

The late lamented Lenah tollhouse

The Arcola tollhouse was no slouch either, taking in over $1,000 a year. It was the last toll on the pike—three and a half miles from Aldie. The only complaints anybody had about the turnpike were that its straight-as-an-arrow construction and its uphill-downhill grades sacrificed easy round-the-hill grades for speed. With the tollhouse in reparable condition, an errant highway department bulldozer took the structure's measure in 1995.

By 1868 the Arcola Post Office on the pike had moved to what everybody called Gum Spring, today's Arcola. Now, there was no area post office, but in 1888, Philip A. Hutchison put Lenah on the map. He had been a strong supporter of Grover Cleveland, who won that year's presidential race against Republican James G. Blaine. The spoils system rewarded Mr. Hutchison by putting a post office in his house. But what should he call it? Little River was the first thought, but Virginia already had a post office with that name. Zion and Mount Zion were second and third choices, but again, there were Commonwealth post offices with those names. Mr. Hutchison didn't have a fourth choice, so out came the sheet of names that the post office department handed to prospective postmasters who couldn't make up their minds about what to call their offices. The list ran about five pages, and most of the names were three to five letters in length as people had trouble spelling.

African names were popular then; talk of the explorers Stanley and Livingston was on everybody's lips. Girls' names were also popular, and maybe Philip once had a girlfriend named Lenah. So Lenah it would be. A year later, in 1889, Eugene W. Presgraves opened a store at the southwest corner of the Little River Turnpike-to-Lenah Road, and the post office moved in with him. Store and post office stayed in his hands for 37 years—up to then the longest continuous tenure for a lower Loudoun County postmaster. In 1914, Mr. Presgraves wasn't feeling too well and thought he'd give over the post office job to his wife, Ida. Ida, however, declined.

During the last decade of the 19th century and first decade of the 20th, other businesses came to the village. George Henry Hutchison ran an undertaking establishment through 1910, and his son Silas took over through the teens. George Henry's daughters, Miss Minnie and Miss Fannie, helped the family by running a millinery shop.

In 1896, Lenah got a schoolhouse, so its children no longer had to walk the often-swampy two and a half miles to the Little River School. Henry M. and Elizabeth A. Smith sold a half-acre lot to the Broad Run District school trustees for $3 on September 24, 1895. The deed specified that the half-acre was to be a "school lot where a white [children's] school is to be taught." Next year the frame one-roomer was built and opened. Among its well-known teachers were Janney Ewell and Hannah Turman. But no one stayed longer than Daisy Hutchison, who was still teaching when the school closed in 1927.

By 1924, Charles A. "Charlie" Whaley from Arcola rented the store from Mr. and Mrs. Presgraves. John "Jack" Hutchison took over from him in 1926, and got the postmastership from Mrs. Presgraves, who held it less than a year after her husband's death. At that time, Lenah was the last stop on what was known as the Ashburn Star Route.

The mail buggy, whipped along by Conway LeFevre, and later

Lacy Ferguson, took mail off the train at Ashburn and carted it to Ryan, Waxpool, Royville, Arcola, and Lenah. The old turnpike (today's Route 50) had been blacktopped in 1922 and 1923, though nobody expected the pavement to last. But last it did. And eventually the Star Route's horses and buggies gave way to a Model A from Aldie, and in 1932 Rural Free Delivery signaled the end of the Lenah Post Office. James Oliver Smith was Lenah's last postmaster. The new postmark was Aldie.

About 1920, Carroll Hutchison, the miller at Aldie, had a frame grist mill built on the north side of the pike, and Stuart Burton ran its gasoline-powered machinery. When the Lenah mill burned down about 1927, Stuart and his wife, Nellie, devoted their energies to running the frame store that he had built east of the mill in 1925. S. O. Burton—as he signed his checks—also sold Gulf gasoline. With such competition from the Burtons just across the pike, Jack Hutchison—courtesy of Standard Oil—put up the village's first sign with the name "Lenah" on it. The sign read "J. H. Hutchison, Lenah, Virginia." Standard Oil did nice things like that for people, as long as they sold its gasoline. Everybody thought it was proper to have "Hutchison" on the sign. It has been said that for at least a half century, anyone could walk along a local road and greet a gentleman stranger with "Good morning, Mr. Hutchison," and eight times out of 10 hit the mark.

Mr. Presgraves's old store, a one-story, frame, gable-roof building with a carriage-high loading deck and lean-to storage wing, burned about 1937, when it was operated by Martin Swart. Four years earlier, Mr. Burton's frame store had also burned, but he built it back in cement block. It closed for the last time in 1940.

In 1935, Carroll Hutchison, who was still working at the Aldie Mill, was able to buy the machinery from the old Bodine Mill near Gainesville in Prince William. Carroll moved the machinery to Lenah and built a gambrel-roofed building to house it. Once again with the help of Stuart Burton, Carroll ran the gristmill, this time from 1936 until 1957. Then it was converted to a house.

As the four lanes of the John Mosby Highway—since 1990 Loudoun's nom-de-plume for Route 50—end just east of Lenah, the village now is a separator—a border settlment between eastern exurbia and western hill country.

Watson

**The Village
Atop Negro
Mountain**

A mile and two-tenths south of Evergreen Mills on the Old Carolina Road the pavement once ended. Here begins Watson, since the
early 1840s known as Negro Mountain, and later, Watson Mountain.
Yardley Taylor placed the name Negro Mountain on his 1853 map of
Loudoun County, for by that time the area was pocketed with small
frame and log homes lived in by Free Negroes.

Some of those homes are gone; others have been covered with
siding. By their foundations are several family graveyards, the stones
unmarked, enveloped by creeper. In the First Baptist churchyard, however, some of the older stones have inscriptions and bear the names of
the old families: Emily Ellen Lee Thornton, born a slave in 1861 and
the daughter of John and Martha Lee, servants of the George Lees of
Farmwell Plantation; Kate Hogan Bowler, born a slave in 1857. The
white Hogans—James William, Nicholas, and Patrick—were overseers
for President James Monroe's Oak Hill plantation.

The mountain reaches nearly 500 feet, and the ridge rises gently
west of the road. Two small streams, tributaries of Goose Creek, parallel the road, one to the east, one to the west. Traditionally, the east
rivulet was Tanyard Branch; the west rivulet was Piney Hill Branch. But
when workmen paved the road in 1957, with tongue in cheek they told
a name-checker making the first U. S. government map of the area that
the streams were called Tan Branch and Black Branch.

In the spring of 1888 the community changed complexion with
the completion of a frame store built for John O. Daniel. On June 12
that year, a post office opened at the store.

The name of the post office was not to be Negro Mountain, but
Watson. In retrospect, the choice of that name appears unusual. The
one person named Watson who owned property in the area was Mrs.
Mary E., with a modest 15 acres in Mercer District. No one named
Watson ever owned a tract of any size on Negro Mountain.

Postmaster John O. Daniel gave the job to kin James O. Daniel in
1889. Ten years later, on July 17, 1899, John O. Daniel and his wife,
Magnolia, sold the "store house, dwelling house and stable" to John

William Mitchell for $1,000. Mr. Daniel had paid $600 for the eight scrub acres in 1889.

Mr. Mitchell did not take over the store immediately, for that January, John O. had leased the property to W. H. Moffett. Eugenia M. Utterback had also assumed the post office duties from James O. Daniel. But by early 1902, at the latest—for Mr. Moffett had a three-year lease— Will Mitchell managed the store. He was to run it until 1956.

In his early years, Mr. Mitchell had continuing battles with the post office department. He became postmaster in 1903, and two years later word came from Washington that there was to be no more Watson Post Office. Folks on Negro Mountain didn't have much clout with the bureaucracy, but Mr. Mitchell won a reprieve. In 1907, when the post office was again designated to close, Mr. Mitchell argued that revenues were sure to increase because he had just put in a telephone. And revenues did increase. But by 1912, when many steady customers began to get their own phones, the post office was discontinued. Shortly, Mitchell's Store became a regular stop on John Virts's RFD route out of Leesburg.

Will Mitchell's phone came courtesy of Dr. Fred Hutchison's Prince William Telephone Company. Mr. Mitchell rented the phone out to his customers, charging them 50 cents a month to use the line. When a customer rang a bell on the phone, the operator would answer; she had the numbers. Aldie was five *short* rings, and Leesburg was one *long*. If nobody answered, the caller had to keep trying. Every phone on the line had a different ring.

The stable mentioned in the 1899 deed was undoubtedly the blacksmith shop that stood north of the store for many years in the early 20th century. "Old Man" Jim Sinclair was the smith during those years, and sometime before 1920, Wes Eidson took over. He was followed in 1926 by Clarence Harris Scott, who ran the shop until the late 1930s. Mr. Scott then moved the business nearer to his new home on Red Hill Road, and there it remained until he retired, about 1955. The Watson shop was moved some 200 feet north and is now a home painted blue.

Watson's one other business was of a later vintage, the Southern States Co-op agency of B. J. Fletcher, which began in 1933. B. J. Fletcher & Son (his son, Gordon, became a partner in 1938) specialized in feed, seed, fertilizer, and farm equipment. In 1940 the business moved out on Route 50 to Lenah.

First Baptist Church of Watson organized in 1896. About a decade later Will Mitchell decided the community needed a church for whites. Ice cream festivals in front of his store paid for some of the building, and he paid for the rest. It was about 1909 that the frame church north of the store was finished. Locals called it Watson Mountain Church because of the twice-monthly afternoon services that were held there. They also called it "The Hall" because it was a community center and social hall. Watson Mountain Church was officially Presbyterian and was on the Aldie-Floris circuit. Services stopped in the late 1930s. Those years also saw the last of the area Watsons: siblings Fannie, Lucy, and Ed. Fannie Watson Utterback was a teacher of long standing at Aldie School.

First Baptist Church of Watson served the black population. The Reverend Douglass D. Fisher organized the church on November 29, 1896, following a number of prayer meetings held in area homes. The organization meeting took place at the home of Edward Moten, about a mile from where the church now stands. Among the charter members were the Reverend Bush W. Murray, Frances Bigsby, Mr. and Mrs. Lewis Hall, Samuel Thornton Jr., Mr. and Mrs. Edward Gant, Mr. and Mrs. George Overall, Rachel Lee, and Martha Dearin.

On July 4, 1898, L. A., Martha, and Virginia Lee sold land to the congregation so that it could build a church. The price was $20, and the deed described the ground: "It lyes near the Watson Post Office upon the Red Hill road." Messrs. Hall, Thornton, and Gant, along with A. Edmunds and A. Fletcher, were the trustees for "the New School Colored Baptist Church near Watson, Virginia." By 1899 a frame church arose. Building it was no easy task in days when area black men earned 75 cents a day and black women 50 cents. The congregation donated much of the labor.

The Reverend Fisher, often called "a fisher of men," served a number of years. The Reverend A. R. Pinkett followed, and under his guidance the church grew. But by 1920 many older members had passed on and many other members had left for the city and its jobs. The Reverend Gillian pastored First Baptist during these hard times.

The Reverend Lindsay C. Murray, son of Bush Murray, and a man who had been baptized by Reverend Fisher in 1903, became pastor in August 1929 and served until 1962. In 1955 the church caught fire from an overheated stove. Only the Bible and pulpit chairs were saved. For two years the congregation worshipped at First Baptist, Sycolin, until the present block building was completed in 1957.

Like so many of the date stones on other Piedmont churches for black people, the one at First Baptist encapsulates the congregation's history: "First Baptist Church Organized November 29, 1896 Rev. D. B. Fisher Rebuilt - 1955 Reverend L. C. Murray." The Reverend James E. Summers followed Reverend Murray in 1963 and served until September 17, 1979.

PHOTO COURTESY *COURAGE, MY SOUL*

The 1957 First Baptist Church near Watson

For most of the black children on Negro Mountain, the church was a partial home six days a week because the building also served as the Watson School. Shortly after the first church was built, the Broad Run District School Board decided a school was needed. But the board didn't have the $400 or $500 to build one, so it rented the church for a nominal sum and promised to build a school when there was enough money. For this remote sector of Broad Run District the money never came. Each Friday, in preparation for the weekend's worship, the desks and equipment were moved to the corner; and each Monday morning, they were moved back into place.

Watson School, as it was called, closed about 1949, shortly after Douglass Elementary in Leesburg opened. The Watson students were bused to Leesburg. Remembered teachers, who often taught 40 to 50 children during the peak winter season, were Arthur Smith, Annie Gray, Rosie Carter, Beatrice Scipio, Charles H. Willis, Esther Randolph, Mary Johnson, Nancy Clarine Cole, Beryl Glymph, and Sarah Evans.

The best-remembered Watson moonshiner was Collis Grayson, whose peach brandy was much in demand among the Middleburg gentry. Mr. Grayson, part Indian, black, and white, had traveled across the Virginia Piedmont with Harry Worcester Smith, the dean of Loudoun and Fauquier foxhunters. "Daddy Smith," Mr. Grayson called him. In Mr. Grayson's later years (he died in 1968 at age 83), he took loving care of many of Watson's horses; he rarely charged for the service.

James Claude "J. C." Church took over the store from Will Mitchell in 1956. As Mr. Church farmed "Churchland" and other family spreads near Watson, his wife, Helen, was usually behind the counter. She died in 1981, he a year later, and they operated "J. C. Church General Merchandise" until their last days. Their daughter, Shirley Church Sindelar, has owned the store since 1982.

Messrs. Daniel and Mitchell would hardly recognize the store now, for its interior has doubled in size. But the addition retains the flavor of the interior wainscoted walls and the exterior carriage-level loading deck. Will Mitchell would be pleased to know that Church's Store is the largest country emporium in Loudoun County.

Willard

There
Long Before
Dulles Airport

Before there was Dulles International Airport there was Willard. The crossroads hamlet sat just east of the southern end of the central Dulles Airport runway. Somewhat paralleling the runway to the east was the Sterling Road, and at Willard it crossed the Willard Road. At the southwest corner of the crossroads was a store, and across from it a school for white children. A half-mile west, just north of Willard Road, stood Shiloh Primitive Baptist Church. Alongside the church to the west was the school for black children. Nine dwellings completed the village.

Samuel Emerson Horn ran the store, and a post office named Willard was established on January 9, 1900, with farmer Harvey W. Cockerille as postmaster. Three years later Frederick W. Bohrer took over the job.

Willard was named to honor Joseph Edward Willard, who at that time was a member of the Virginia House of Delegates from Fairfax County. The village was so close to the Fairfax line that some residents didn't know what county they were in. Joseph's father, Joseph Clapp Willard, had owned the Willard Hotel in Washington, D. C. The younger Mr. Willard was spoken of as the richest man in Virginia, and locals who passed his two-story frame, 14-bedroom, 50-acre estate in Fairfax town confirmed that assertion. This Mr. Willard became Virginia's lieutenant governor in 1901, but after he came in third in the three-way 1905 race for the top office, he settled for a position as state corporation commissioner.

The fortunes of the Willard Post Office followed that of its namesake. Fred Bohrer closed the window on April 30, 1907, and the Rural Free Delivery carriers from Herndon and Sterling took over.

South along the Sterling Road, Ernest Beard's buggy dropped off the mail, stopping at Coleman's Corner where the old Ox Road crossed, and where the Coleman graveyard stood. Philip J. Coleman's 700-plus-acre spread surrounded the crossroads. He achieved local fame as Broad Run supervisor, school board member, and kingpin of the Democrats of east Loudoun. Next were Tom Underwood's fields. He owned one of the area's two threshing machines. Then came Coleman's School on the land of Eugene Edgar Beard, no relation to Ernest Beard. Eugene was a dairy farmer and newcomer to the area in 1906.

Then you came to one of William Creighton's three spreads, and to dentist Fred Keller's dairy farm; people marveled at how he could pull the udders of 75 cows each morning and then pull teeth. Then it was south to Walter Slough's farm; about 1916 he sold out to Walter F. Watson, teacher and later principal of Sterling School. Then south to the John Paul Woods' place and to Matthew Middleton's dairy farm.

South of Willard crossroads there was Phil Sowers's place (hence old Sowers' Road) and Dr. James Garfield Blevins's spread. Blevins, who also gave his name to Blevins Road, came up from Wythe County in 1910 and practiced dentistry in Pleasant Valley. Adjoining Doc Blevins was the farm of his brother, Marion Blevins. He knew Loudoun County better than anyone, except perhaps Miss Bess Ott, the county nurse of the thirties and forties. And people would joke that Miss Ott followed the second "Doc" Blevins around, for Marion Blevins was a W. T. Raleigh agent, and all of Loudoun was his sole territory. You name the patent medicine—pills, extract, powders for man and beast, he carried them all, first on horseback, then in a Ford truck—for a half century in all, even after he moved to Lincoln in 1945. Around Willard crossroads the farms were smaller. Here lived former slaves and their descendants: Joe Johnson, Joe Jones, Charles Newman, Eldridge Smith, Arthur Thomas, Lafayette and Henry Robinson, and Nathaniel Corum. Nat had a morphine habit, picked up at Horn's store, where, like everywhere else in Loudoun, it was sold over the counter until 1912. Then, morphine had to be prescribed, so Nat traveled once a week to Dr. Walter Russell's in Herndon for his fix from the understanding doctor.

On their few acres these men farmed at a subsistence level: a patch of corn, a large vegetable garden, some chickens and hogs, a cow, a heifer, perhaps a steer. They also worked as hands for the Colemans, Middletons, and Creightons. To make a few extra dollars they cut wood and fashioned it into barrel staves, railroad ties, and ax and hatchet handles. In addition they built their homes, church, and perhaps even their school.

The focus of black Willard was not at the crossroads, but at the church called Shiloh. Its congregation is thought to have first met at the Willard School for black children. Elder James Farr, from Cub Run Primitive Baptist Church at Centreville, was the first known preacher at Shiloh Primitive Baptist, often called just the Willard Church. In 1899 the congregation built a weatherboard building, and two years later, at age 21, Elder James Bailey of Occoquan became part-time pastor, a position he held until 1976, a year before his death. His 75-year tenure—during which he pastored several area churches— must be a record of sorts.

There were four schools for white children, the oldest being Bear's School, still standing on the gentle rise of Stony Hill on the Moran Road (now officially and incorrectly named "Old Ox Road"). The school was named for A. Joseph Bear and his wife, Kate, who donated land for the school in December 1874. The Bears lived to the east in the fine 1803 home remodeled by builder and bootlegger Earl Batt. Bear's School closed about 1910. An older Bear's School stood across the road.

Coleman's School, if built before 1894, stood on lands donated by Joseph and Jane Miller, and if built between 1894 and 1906 stood on land given by John T. and Marie J. Milstead. But the school was not named for the Millers or the Milsteads. Since the Colemans owned nearly all of the land in Willard ex-

cept this 50-acre tract, Coleman's School it became. Remembered teachers were Virginia Andes; Lucy Rogers; Virginia Hutchison; Ruth Coleman from the Eastern Shore and no relation to the Loudoun family; Eugenia Anderson; and Edith Watson and her father, Walter F. Watson. Walter probably closed its doors in the early 1930s. Bulldozers pushed the school down in 1960.

The 1920 Carter's School remains, circa 1985

Carter's School, nearly in ruins when I last saw it, stands on Sowers Road—the county has mistakenly named the way Bears School Road. Carter's School was built about 1920 on Robert Carter's land, and before it closed about 1936 there were teachers Glennie Marshall from

Arcola, Charlotte Weedon from Waterford, Mary Craun from Middleburg, and Mary E. Hemsley, an excellent pianist from Boyce. Walter F. Watson taught from about 1916 until the school closed. The building, weatherboard, but painted white, was probably constructed about the time Willard Post Office opened. A deed to the land has not been found.

Across the road from the school once stood a store that Edward Newman Fitzhugh and his wife, Gussie, operated from 1913 until about 1930, when it closed. The Fitzhughs were married in 1913 at the Eugene Beard place near Coleman's Schoolhouse. Neighbors fashioned wedding wreaths from honeysuckle growing on the road banks. The Fitzhughs were childless, and so they were parents to all schoolchildren, giving them penny candy. And as they lived upstairs from their store, one could count on the gracious Fitzhughs to open up at a customer's beck and call.

Another constant friend to Willard area children was Miss Annie Middleton, who lived at the southeast corner of Willard crossroads. Known as "the Angel of Willard," she was the soother of a hurt finger, the preparer of lunch for a child who forgot to bring his. Late in life she married a Mr. Brogden.

About a half-mile west of the Willard Church stood the Croson place. Here lived Miss Flora Croson, last of the home switchboard operators of Gales Hutchison's Prince William Telephone Company. About 1920 she took over the job from Laura Middleton, daughter of farmer Arthur Middleton, whose house stood on the northeast corner of the Willard and Sowers Roads. Laura's switchboard was known as "The Central," and one long ring brought her to your receiver..

That was Willard, and by the late 1930s, except for Shiloh Church, the houses and vacant schools and store, there was no more.

Then came the airport, Blue Ridge Airport, that is—some 15 years the senior and predecessor of Dulles. West of the Sterling Road and a mile north of the Willard crossroads, for about $50 a month, Harry A. Sager Jr., leased enough land from Otho Kirkwood to clear two strips for landing, in the shape of an "x", each a half-mile long. Mr. Sager had learned to fly when he was at Herndon High School, taking lessons from George Brinkerhoff at the oldest of area airports, College Park in Maryland. Mr. Sager wanted to be an airline pilot, needed the required flying time, and achieved his goal via three second-hand airplanes—a Piper Cub, J-2, bought for $300 ($1,000 new), then a Piper J-3, and a Stinson MS8-A. There were two hangers and the Blue Ridge Flying Club shack.

Harry Sager's Blue Ridge Airport, chartered by the U.S. in 1938, was the county's first official airport. However, it had been preceded by a good two decades by Wallace George's airfield, paralleling the south side of Edwards' Ferry Road, just east of Leesburg. Mr. Sager had chosen the name Blue Ridge because the range comes into view at the site.

When Mr. Sager left Blue Ridge for Eastern Airlines in the spring of 1941, he rented out the field to a Mr. Germaine, manager of Hybla Valley airfield in southern Fairfax County. In those pre-National Airport days (before June, 1941), Hybla Valley was the next fuel stop south of Franklin Reid's Beacon Airport in Alexandria. At Beacon, Arthur Godfrey learned to fly, and hence named his Loudoun home Beacon Hill.

In early 1942 Blue Ridge Airport closed because war-time decrees specified either a twenty-four-hour guard over all airplanes, or removal of the propellors at night.

Beginning in 1948, seven years after National Airport opened, the Civil Aeronautics Administration began exploring three sites for a Washington-area international airfield: Burke, Annandale and Willard (called the Chantilly site because of the Chantilly Post Office in Fairfax). In the summer of 1951 the CAA settled on Burke, but Fairfax Countians would have no part of it, and that, plus expanding Washington suburbs and the CAA's insecurity in regard to its decision, led them to back off. Through 1957 Friendship Airport, Andrews Air Force Base, and Pender were suggested as alternate sites for the field.

In January, 1958, President Dwight D. Eisenhower selected the site named Chantilly; in reality he took the recommendation of Presidential Assistant Edward R. (Pete) Quesada, a World War II fighter-pilot commander.

At that time Harry Sager who had become Eastern Airlines' senior pilot, wrote the CAA and suggested that Chantilly Airport be named Blue Ridge Airport. Pete Quesada, however, demurred and Chantilly Airport it remained until June 1959, when Mr. Quesada, recalling the Secretary of State's fondness for flying, picked Dulles. John Foster Dulles had died the previous month. Then the Secretary's staff, hoping to fore-stall alternate suggestions, took pains to research a total of 556,988 miles logged by their old boss—400,000 out of the country, they added.

Civil Action 1638-M, the government order condemning all property within the confines of some 8,000 acres, should not have been a surprise. The first condemnation letters were dated September 8, 1958. A Washington speculator, Colonel Cy Morehouse, had approached several Willard-area landowners that year offering to buy properties. But there had been no public hearing and the letters came like a bolt.

Landowners formed a citizens association, but it disbanded and everyone followed a separate course, many hiring Washington-area lawyers who for a fee would take one-third of what they could get over the

PHOTO COURTESY LOUDOUN DEPT. OF ECONOMIC DEVELOPMENT

Eero Saainen's "bird-in-flight" terminal building at Dulles Airport

condemnation price. The average taking price was $500 an acre, with small landowners and owners of more than 50 acres getting the best deals. Between January 9, 1959, and April 6, 1961, some 87 property owners deeded the U. S. Government 9,800 acres, the 1,800 acres having been an aftersight because original airport plans failed to allow for certain wind conditions. Eero Saarinen's "bird-in-flight" teminal build-ing—"the best thing I have ever done," said the architect— was built on the 27.1-acre tract of Gerald Donald Popovich and his wife Alda, daughter of teacher-principal Walter F. Watson. They were offered $22,250 for their land enhanced by a four-bedroon Cape Cod home.

The property had been appraised at $43,000, but in court the federal lawyers were able to knockdown the price to $21,500. In all, the federal takings were fraught with inequities and only increased Loudoun's innate distrust of the federal government.

Willard 's durable survivor, Second Shiloh Baptist Church moved to land on Gum Spring Road, just north of Byrnes's Crossroads, on land donated by Isaiah Allen.

The Loudoun County Board of Supervisors, J. Emory Kirkpatrick of Broad Run District, and Dr. William P. Frazer, Jim Arnold, Joshua

Second Shiloh Baptist, in its new home   PHOTO COURTESY *COURAGE, MY SOUL*

Fletcher, and J. Terry Hirst, were not for the airport, but they could do nothing. Two days before President John F. Kennedy's November 17, 1962, dedication of Dulles, Terry Hirst summed up the board's feelings: "Yes, industry pays taxes, big taxes—to the state and federal governments. It'll be the county that pays for the population boom."

Virginia's big push during the 1960s, though, was to search for industry, and Terry Hirst's remarks, stated many times, were lost in this last era of low taxes, a country school system, and a county government unable to fathom the consequences of urbanization.

With little air traffic in Dulles's first years, people seemed more concerned wih changing the airport's name than for planning around it. Governor Albertis Harrison supported a move to rename Dulles. He and many others felt it should be Washington International Airport.

That name came to the fore when sloppy speech and garbled public address announcements mixed up "Dulles" with "Dallas." More than one passenger had deplaned in Loudoun thinking she was in Texas. So, when the airport's 20th anniversary came up, and Winn Porter asked me to draw a map of the land within thirty minutes' driving time of the airport, he asked me to think of a new name. Mr. Porter, of Paeonian Springs, was on the airport's governing board. I picked Washington Dulles International Airport, and the U. S. Congress followed suit a few years later.

And of that old name, Willard, I recall overhearing a conversation at some airport event a decade-or-so ago. A man asked an African American hostess, "Just where are we?" For a moment she hesitated, and then with a knowing smile replied, "At Willard, of course."

PHOTO COURTESY LOUDOUN COUNTY DEPT.OF ECONOMIC DEVELOPMENT

*Willard, Virginia,
today*

Waxpool

Reverend
Popkins'
Domain

If a circle were drawn with Leesburg, Aldie, and Sterling on its circumference, the center of that circle would be Waxpool—just about in the middle of eastern Loudoun. Few people notice the 20 or so houses of this village, spaced along the westernmost mile of the dusty lane reaching from Ryan to Mount Hope Church.

The church, though not Waxpool's first, nurtured the community for many years and indirectly brought about its name. Storekeeper James H. Wrenn, noting, as did nearly everyone, that the hard-to-drain clay-loam soils (technically called Iredell-Mecklenburg) were the area's dominant feature, proposed the name "Waxpool" and forwarded his suggestion to the Reverend George W. Popkins for approval. As we shall

PHOTO COURTESY LOUDOUN HERITAGE FARM MUSEUM

Wrenn's store at Waxpool, just a short time ago

see, the reverend's approval in such matters was always needed.

The church where Reverend Popkins was pastor had its beginnings in the controversies regarding salvation that embroiled Baptists of the 1830s—was a baptized person saved through baptism? The Reverends Thaddeus Herndon and William F. Broaddus of Culpeper County organized Mount Hope Church on August 24, 1835.

Seven charter members—James Keen, Robert H. Cochran, Henry Ball, Christopher Houser, Edward Tillett, Lucinda Chappel, and Susan Tillett—chose Thaddeus Herndon for their pastor. The location of their church is no longer known, though some point to the stone Red Hill School (now the wing of the John Wallace home east of Watson). Others point to the old Broad Run Church.

Broad Run Church was the first house of worship in the Waxpool area, and its first mention was in July 1757, when the church was the termination point of several roads. A June 9, 1766, deed from Kitchen and Ann Prim to John Pyles noted that from his 600 acres "about one Acre [would be] Excepted out of this Grant where the Church stands." Use of the word "Church" without an affixed denomination and instead of "Meetinghouse" implies that Broad Run Church was Anglican. If so, it was the oldest Anglican church in the county—the 1736 "Chapel Above Goose Creek" north of Leesburg was but a Chapel of Ease, a chapel not attended by a regular minister. Old-timers from the Waxpool-Ryan area, though, recall hearing that Broad Run Church was Presbyterian. So, like the Gum Spring Church at Arcola, this church might have been used by followers of different faiths.

When the site went up for sale in 1803, it was called "Old Broad Run Church Tract," and there is an 1879 deed that mentions a road from "the old church to Daysville." Although the whereabouts of the first Mount Hope Church aren't known, the Broad Run Church's location has been pinpointed, thanks—in a sense—to Earl Smith, who inadvertently dug up part of its graveyard while building his barn in the late 1930s. The graveyard is on the old LeFevre tract, less than a mile east of Waxpool, and has been preserved as a focal point for a park in the Broadlands development.

Between May 1852 and October 1853 a new Mount Hope Church was built on its present site. The location was then described as "on the corner of the widow Mills' dower land where the Gum spring road crosses the old church road." Mrs. Mills was Elizabeth Mills, and the "Gum spring road" is today's Belmont Ridge Road. The old church road is now the Waxpool Road. Members and neighbors hauled lumber for the building, and during construction the congregation worshipped at the stone Red Hill School. A high point in the church's spiritual growth came with an eight-day service in early September 1854.

In 1877 a schoolhouse named Mount Hope joined the church. Mount Hope School became a two-roomer shortly after 1900, but through most of its life only one of the rooms was used. Remembered teachers were Mary Frame, Susie Bitzer (Walker), Nona Parks, May Barrow, Virginia Hutchison, Eva Cross, Laura Hunt (Cross), Lillian Moran (Ball), Julia Newman, and a Miss Campbell. Professor Harry Daniel from Evergreen Mills closed the school's doors in the fall of 1933, and next spring Boyer Phillips drove students on the area's first school bus to Ashburn School.

Widower Walter Poland then bought the schoolhouse, and throughout the 1930s he held dances there that were eastern Loudoun fixtures. The school burned in the 1950s.

On July 23, 1878, thirteen members of the Mills family donated the acre and a half that Mount Hope had been standing on for a quarter-century to the church's board of trustees. The present German-siding Mount Hope Church replaced the 1853 structure in 1893. While it was being built, the congregation met in the Mount Hope School.

In early 1886, Pastor George Washington Popkins, whose farm lay just east of Waxpool, had nearly completed his 10th year at Mount Hope. No other Mount Hope pastor had served as long. Acquaintances say Popkins was "born a politician," and from the pulpit he often said that he was a statesman as well as a preacher. Every year, on Homecoming Day, the second Sunday in June, Reverend Popkins invited well-known congressmen and senators to address the congregation after the luncheon feast. Through such men he had become a guide at the White House. Pastor Popkins received no salary for being a guide, but with the tips he earned, he was able to afford a town house on Chapman Street in D. C. Each Sunday evening a parishioner took Pastor Popkins by buggy to the Ashburn Station, and he rode the train and the streetcar into Washington. Each Friday evening he reversed the trip. After G. W. Popkins died in 1931, Mount Hope parishioners lost their fervor for Homecoming Day.

Despite at least one attempt to remove Reverend Popkins as preacher, he served Mount Hope until the end of his life. His 53-year ministry remains a Loudoun record. Reverend Popkins also shepherded the Baptist churches at Ashburn and Sterling during that tenure.

No doubt it was Pastor Popkins who thought of the idea for a local post office, asked storekeeper Jim Wrenn to come up with a name for one, and then approved Mr. Wrenn's choice of Waxpool. Official records give the post's establishment as April 15, 1886. Mr. Wrenn became postmaster in his store, which he rented from Samuel Edgar Munday.

During this time and through the early years of the 20th century, Ben Hurst, brother of Will Hurst, who ran the store at Ryan, was the Waxpool blacksmith. His shop was located at the northeast corner of the Waxpool and Belmont Ridge Roads. Ben and Civil War veteran

Robert Sowers were vocal critics of Reverend Popkins's rather blatant politicizing from the pulpit. Mr. Sowers used to say, "Find out how Popkins is voting, vote opposite, and you vote right." Ben is remembered for a remark he made coming off a hung jury: "Eleven of the orneriest men I ever saw."

The second Samuel Edgar Munday, son of Samuel Edgar Munday, became storekeeper and postmaster of Waxpool in 1909. He served as postmaster until February 1, 1940. "Ed" Munday didn't have the use of his legs and walked with two canes. But he could "do more than most men," running a farm as well as the store. Cornelius Jenkins helped him behind the counter in the teens, son Lawrence Munday helped out in the 1920s, and son James and daughter Tessie Penn assisted in later years. Ed's brother, Ernest Leonard Munday, was the Ashburn storekeeper.

An attempt to get rid of the waxy soil that made the Waxpool Road nearly impassable half the year caught the area's fancy in the early 1920s. They say nearly $1,000 was raised, mostly from 50-cent and one-dollar contributions, to macadamize the mile stretch from Belmont Ridge

PHOTO COURTESY LOUDOUN HERITAGE FARM MUSEUM
Front view of the Wrenn-Munday-Tillett store at Waxpool

Road to Church Spring Branch at Alexander's Corner. Will J. Hay, the Ashburn road commissioner, supervised the project, and Ralph Bitzer's Fordson tractor pulled the rock crusher that pulverized the big stones.

Tessie Penn Munday Tillett became Waxpool postmistress on February 19, 1940. And though she closed the store in 1944 because gas rationing had reduced the number of customers, she continued as postmistress until May 31, 1950. On that date, the post office was discontinued on orders from President Dwight D. Eisenhower. It was the last of the old posts to close in eastern Loudoun.

In 2001, Bill Tillett donated the still-intact contents of the old store to the Loudoun Heritage Farm Museum at Claude Moore Park.

Royville

On The
Way To
Brambledown

"Chaney Hough, poor old Chaney," was Beulah Franklin Sowers's refrain whenever the subject of the Houghs came up. The Houghs, to all, were "Mr. and Mrs. Royville." Royville was a hamlet of two, maybe three homes, located two miles north of Arcola, on the road to Mount Hope Church and Belmont Park. Once it was the land of the Odens, Freemans, and Lees, but by the 1890s there were mostly Hutchisons and Sowerses.

It couldn't have been too many years before 1890 when Roy Hough died of typhoid fever. He was 14. His mother, Ella Hough, opened the Royville Post Office in 1893. She and her husband owned 27 acres at the village crossroads. The road east went to Lee Thompson's dairy farm and then hooked into the old Arcola-to-Sterling-Road by Carter's Schoolhouse. Going west, the road at one time had continued into Red Hill, but in the 1890s it was a lane into the woods where black people lived—Carrie Nickens, and Dick and Norvell Overhall.

No one remembers when the Houghs opened their store, but it was located right at their combination home and post office at the northwest corner of the crossroads. A rural post office was a good way to bring in extra customers, and besides, Ella had a green thumb. In early spring people would come from Arcola, Waxpool, and Ryan to buy her hotbed plants.

In 1895 after remodeling their business, the Houghs found themselves in debt to American Home Building and Loan. For 15 years it was like that. They mortgaged their property repeatedly to secure debts to the Herndon Milling Company, C. C. Saffer's Leesburg mill, storeowner Harris Levy, Rachel A. Little, and others—"poor old Chaney," as Beulah Sowers said.

Chaney was Ella Hough's husband. John C. C. Hough was his real name—and which "C" stood for Chaney probably no one will ever know. The store was always in her name, "Ella A. Hough & Co." Mr. Hough kept the business going by doing custom farming. Once he even had to mortgage the animals (mules and horses) and the tools (an

Evans corn planter, Deering one-horse mower, McCormick mower, corn binder, two Malta cultivators, a three-horse plow, two harrows, and a two-horse wagon) of his trade.

There was a school at Royville, about two-thirds of a mile north of the store. Lavolette Sowers was the last and only remembered teacher. Students called her "Miss Lav." Her uncle, the Reverend Nathaniel O. Sowers, had given her the name Lavolette. He had taught at an Indian reservation in Missouri and learned the name there.

The school was called Brambleton because Brambleton was the name of the Hutchison farm on which the building stood. The name is pronounced *bramble-down,* but Brambleton was an old Hutchison family name. The school closed in 1912 and has been a private home ever since.

The end had also come to Royville. The post office closed in 1910, and Ella Hough died in 1913. Three years later the Hough's home and store burned. L. B. "Billy" Creighton came to the crossroads about 1914. He was a midwesterner and had a dairy farm near Herndon. He bought the Lee Thompson dairy farm and converted it into a stock farm, raising sheep and cattle. People said Billy was from Scotland and he pronounced his name *cry-ton.* He had the area's first auto, an open Velie touring car, with a big trunk in back.

About 1932, when the state was preparing the first county highway map, it called Billy's road Creighton Road, and Royville it called Creighton Corner. There are still remains of the Creighton place, though the house burned down about 1950. The road, a dead end for more than four decades, bears the Creighton name.

Another story about Royville survives. First, one has to be introduced to Will Overhall. He was a black man, orphaned by chance or choice after the Civil War and raised by Bob Sowers, a Confederate veteran. Bob taught Will to read and write, and also to farm. By 1900 Will was one of the area's best farmers. He was a "high-type" man, as whites called cultured blacks, and he was also a musician.

In Will's youth he often threw in with the young white men of the area, and one evening a bunch of them went down to Arcola to hear a preaching at the Methodist Church. They had walked passed the Royville store when one of the fellows asked Will—who was known to have quite an arm—if he could throw a rock over the store. Will accepted the challenge, but lost the bet. Next day he stopped by the store and was confronted by Chaney Hough. "Will, I hear there's quite a preaching down at Arcola. You should go."

"Mr. Hough," Will replied, "we went down there the other night."

"That's all I want to know," said Hough. "You owe me for a broken window."

Lunette

Is There
Buried Gold
At The S-curve?

Most people around Lunette today will tell you that it's on the Braddock Road, and that's what they still call it in Fairfax County. But people around Lunette were calling dusty Route 620 the Braddock Road more than a century before Fairfax County put up its road signs in the late 1960s.

Historians will tell you that the misnaming of the Braddock Road, which roughly paralleled Route 7, came from W. H. Snowden's misreading of surveyor John Dalrymple's notes on British Major General Braddock's 1755 expedition against the French and Indians. But Mr. Snowden's 1902 book, *Young Surveyors,* was so popular that people tended to take for granted its claim that Route 620 was the Braddock Road—despite contrary evidence that became available by the early 1920s.

At that time, few area folk about Lunette, Arcola, and Conklin had heard of W. H. Snowden. To them, the Braddock Road story began sometime after the War of 1812, with a search for buried treasure.

Nobody had ever heard much about General Braddock and his ill-fated journey to Fort Duquesne until some unremembered year after the second war with Great Britain. A group of Englishmen from London came to Alexandria one day with a map showing the location of a cache of gold coins, buried just southwest of an S-curve on a dirt track then called the Colchester Road. They were secretive about what they were after, but they knew that before they could dig for the coins, they had to tell the story to certain landowners along the road.

But the English treasure seekers didn't tell area folk the full story. You see, the $25,000-to-$30,000-worth of gold coins had been poured into the muzzles of two brass cannon, and the cannon would be easy to find—especially since a Braddock document in the British Museum had described the cannons and site: "buried with muzzles upward, wooden plug in each. Two feet under. Fifty paces east of a spring, where the road runs north and south."

The Englishmen didn't mention the amount of gold—then worth more than a million—the cannon, or that the road ran "north and south." Instead they just mentioned the S-curve and told the overall story: When

Sir Peter Halkett's men of Braddock's force had marched west from Alexandria, a party with a payroll followed them. To discourage robbers, however, the payroll party took a different route than the Vestal's Gap Road. They took the Colchester Road. When this party reached Carter lands in eastern Loudoun, there were rumors that they were going to be bushwhacked by brigands. So they buried some gold coins and split up, later reuniting at a camp northwest of Winchester. As Sir Peter was then in somewhat of a hurry to get to Fort Duquesne, he told the party to leave the cache and dig it up after their return. The return never came, but the map and the regimental orderly book found their way back to England.

The English visitors telling the story some 90 years later dug up every S-curve outside of Alexandria, and as they reached into western Fairfax, one of the Carters got wind of what they were after. This Mr. Carter lived at the brick house, today called Lunette, and when he heard the story, he recollected that less than a quarter-mile south of his home, the original Colchester Road was shaped like an "S" where it straddled the small ridge and bottom lands through Foley's and Dry Weather Branches. In fact, the road went by the old Carter graveyard.

Dead sure that this was the "S" the Englishmen were talking about, Mr. Carter kept mum when the gentlemen from London showed him the map. And because the road straightened out west of Dry Weather Branch, the Englishmen soon gave up their search and returned to London.

Well, John Moran Byrne, who got this story from Ted Linton, who bought the house from the Carters, never felt it appropriate to ask how much digging Mr. Carter did. Mr. Linton never dug, nor did Mr. Byrne, nor did his son, Fred. But they all passed down the story of the map, the S-curve, and the supposed treasure site.

The name Lunette may have come in during the Civil War, for at the time, popular usage of the word referred to a two-sided fortification, generally earth, shaped like a "V." Lunettes often guarded vantage points along roads and river crossings, and it's a good bet there was a lunette by the Carter house during the war.

In 1894, or early 1895, Charles Ashby (Frank) Thomas built a two-story frame building to the west of the old brick Carter house and started up a general store and post office. The post office, established in 1895, was called Lunette. As the word went against the government's general policy that post office names could be no more than five letters long, Mr. Thomas must have had a strong reason for choosing the unusual name. By that time the most common definition of *lunette* was a crescent moon.

About five years later, Mr. Thomas built a gasoline-powered gristmill west of the store. Jim Pearson took over the mill's operation, grinding feed and making meal. The one-story, one-room frame mill ran until 1911, when it was torn down.

In 1904, Edwin H. Harris took over the Lunette store and postmastership, and in 1906, Randall McGaha Barton became postmaster. To most, it seemed that Mr. Pearson ran the post office, because Mr. Barton was always farming. Mr. Pearson also ran the store for a year after Mr. Harris gave up the business in 1910. The Lunette Post Office was discontinued on July 31, 1907, when Rural Free Delivery came in and the mails were dropped off at Arcola.

Late in 1911, Theodore Linton moved the store onto his farm and converted it into a granary. It burned along with a barn when it was struck by lightning in 1942. Even the ever-flowing water of Dry Weather Branch couldn't put out the flames.

The neighborhood went without a business until June of 1920, when Frank Byrne, who previously worked at Charles Maffett's store in Arcola, opened a small frame store at Byrne's Cross Roads, so named because Frank owned all four corners of the Braddock and the Gum Spring Roads. Frank's store closed about 1946, when gas rationing ended after World War II and people could drive once again to the larger stores at Arcola.

Mahala

**Where
Miss Annie
Was Mistress**

Through the years, Mahala has been known by three names. The first was Frankville, in use from the 1840s through the early 20th century, though no family named Frank owned property in the separate area. Frankville consisted of at least three buildings, one of them possibly a store, at the intersection of the Leesburg and Alexandria Turnpike (today's Route 7) and what was then called the Ox Road or Farmwell Road (today's Ashburn Road).

On October 29, 1884, Thomas H. Rose bought two acres "near Frankville" at the southeast corner of the "Leesburg and Alexandria Turnpike" and "Ox Road" that included a "dwelling house and out buildings." Shortly thereafter, he opened a store that stood at the southeast corner. The store was frame, one and a half stories, with a gently peaked roof, and in 1894 it became home of a new post office called Mahala.

Mahala was a popular girl's name of the period, and it might have been the name of one of Thomas Rose's children or of someone else in his family. Locally, most people pronounced the name *ma-hay-lee*. They quickly took to the pronunciation, and the name Frankville was erased from everywhere but the deeds.

For a business, Mr. Rose's location was not as good as it would have been before the Civil War. Farmville (today's Ashburn) had a railroad, but it was two miles away. And the Ox Road (named because it was wide enough for an oxcart), once one of the main east-west roads of Loudoun and Fairfax, had lost most of its cargo when the Leesburg Turnpike was put through in about 1820.

In 1884 there were two business centers at Mahala. The second center was about a mile west of Mr. Rose's store. Here, at the site of the first Belmont Post Office (opened in 1838), stood a blacksmith shop and, just west of it, a wheelwright shop. This second business center stood opposite a large square-frame farm manager's house erected about 1895 for Frederick P. Stanton, former Tennessee Congressman, and owner of Belmont. The house was torn down in 1975.

Jim Horsman operated the blacksmith shop, and George Solomon ran the wheelwright shop. George had two sisters, Margaret and Betty, both of whom lived back in "The Pines." That was the local name for the old Coton plantation (today's Xerox training center), where there were some tenant farms. In winter Margaret and Betty's cattle would often stray onto the pike. Their neighbors Pete and Fred Dove, whose parents, Elizabeth Miller Dove and her husband, William, owned 101 acres of good Goose Creek bottomland, regularly rescued the cattle. And because Pete and Fred knew how poor the sisters were, they would always feed the animals before returning them home.

In 1908, John Guthrie Hopkins, the Greenwich, Connecticut, mining magnate, had both shops taken down, shortly after he bought the Coton tract. He also relocated the Solomon sisters nearer to Ashburn.

Mahala's post office closed on January 15, 1906, and the old Ashburn Star Route gave way to Rural Free Delivery out of the Ashburn Post Office. Thomas Rose's store, however, lingered on and actually got a shot in the arm in 1911 with the formation of the Leesburg & Washington Good Roads Association, Inc.

The association was the idea of banker and ex-druggist Robert N. Harper. Mr. Harper had made a pile with a patent medicine called Caradoc, and he was a director of Riggs National Bank. His substantial brick home, named Caradoc Hall—not for the medicine, but for the knight of King Arthur's Round Table—wasn't more than 10 feet from the dusty old pike; and one of the first things the Good Roads Association did was spend $7,000 to move the pike away from Caradoc Hall.

The Good Roaders' purpose was "to repair, reconstruct, grade and Macademize [sic]...the public road known as the Leesburg and Georgetown Turnpike...from Leesburg to Langley, Fairfax County." The list of its directors reads like a Loudoun who's who of 90 years ago: H. H. Trundle, F. E. Saunders, W. B. Hibbs, E. B. White, and E. G. Rust, all of Leesburg or nearby; W. C. Eustis of Oatlands; Henry Fairfax of Oak Hill; W. T. C. Rogers, John G. Hopkins, J. G. Hutchison of Ashburn; J. V. Nichols of Purcellville; and Robert R. Walker of Waterford. And to show that there was no partiality toward Loudouners, Mr. Harper included two directors from Fairfax: W. E. Lynn of Langley and Mark Turner of Forestville (today's Great Falls).

In 1912 the Good Roaders put up a tollgate about 300 feet east of Mr. Rose's Mahala store. There hadn't been a tollgate on the Leesburg

Pike since 1891, when the second postwar Goose Creek bridge (at Route 7) was built. Back in May of 1889 the Johnstown flood had swept away the 1870 covered bridge, and within the next two years a tollgate was put up at the site where the Stanton farm manager's house would later be—so it could catch the traffic from the temporary ferry and from the railroad depot at Belmont Park. As expected, the toll lasted until after a new bridge was built, but it had stopped by the time the Mahala Post Office opened in 1894. Some say that Mr. Solomon and Mr. Horsman had opened their wheelwright and blacksmith shops opposite this tollgate because they thought it would never close.

The new tollgate that the Good Roaders put up in 1912 was open from dawn to dusk and was operated by Annie Virginia Downs, a widow. On the porch of the small frame house where she lived, rested a pole anchored by a rope. On the other end of the pole was a weight, and when the weight was released, the pole came up to let a horse or wagon by. The standard fee for a vehicle was 10 cents, and when autos came in, they were charged 25 cents. Horses went through free, as did doctors and ministers, and there were no tolls to or from church on Sunday. Considering that the Leesburg tollgate, just east of where Market and Loudoun Streets meet, was only four miles west and the Broad Run tollhouse three miles east, travelers avoided the pike, even though travel got a bit cheaper: the state took the tolls off at Broad Run in 1924.

Miss Annie's tollhouse.   PHOTO COURTESY LOUDOUN TIMES-MIRROR

Annie Downs, however, exacted the maximum from each carrier that went down the pike. They say she could hear an auto a mile off, and as one approached the rise at Mahala, she'd be out in the center of the road, hands on her hips and looking right at the driver.

President Warren G. Harding was a good friend of the Edward B. McLeans, who had bought Belmont in 1915. When Mr. Harding first visited Belmont, his presidential motorcade of two autos had bumped the 30 miles from the White House without paying a single toll. But when the presidential autos reached Mahala, there was Miss Annie, out in the center of Leesburg Pike with her familiar posture.

The secret service man in the motorcade's first car stopped and smilingly asked Miss Annie if she didn't know who the gentleman in the backseat was. Miss Annie looked, shrugged, and countered that she was not paid to recognize people but to collect tolls. So President Harding went to his wallet, a ritual he repeated throughout the years of his trips to Belmont. His forays were many, as Evalyn Walsh McLean arranged for the president to meet his lady friends at the estate.

Next door, Thomas and Sarah Rose had sold their store and dwelling lot, described as "at Frankville," to Robert Harper's Washington-to-Leesburg Turnpike Company on July 26, 1915. The selling price was $400. Dick Downs, Annie's son, then kept the Mahala store, with his sister Tillie sometimes helping out.

The state of Virginia took over Robert Harper's turnpike, at least the Loudoun-to-Dranesville section, in 1928 and officially renamed the road Route 54. The state paved the road and took off the tollhouses. The one at Mahala was the last to go. On April 22, 1930, the old turnpike company sold the store and the two-acre tollhouse lot to Annie Downs for $1,500. She and son Dick tore down the store and put up the first gas station on the pike the same year. They sold three brands of gas, and slowly the name Ashburn Junction crept in. People just couldn't pronounce Mahala anymore.

Broad Run Farms
An Eden Still

The late Jim Birchfield would have approved of my dividing the Broad Run article. When I first submitted the piece to him—he was then editor of the *Loudoun Times-Mirror*—it ran 18 pages of typed copy. "Who's going to read all that stuff?" he said. Then he leafed through it and commented: "We're paying you $15 an article. I guess I will have to raise it to $25." That was in late June 1976.

Robert Barnes Young, a lawyer for the U. S. Senate, and his wife, Barbara Fellows Young, bought the 706-acre Miskel farm in 1950. Then it was remote and part of another world, bounded by woods and two-lane Route 7, commonly called Leesburg Pike. Broad Run, scenic and winding, was readily visible from the humpbacked stone bridge, built in 1820, that carried the pike across the run's wide waters. The only sign of modernity was a "second" Route 7, built in 1948 to the north of the old pike. The road had a white line down the center and crossed Broad Run on a concrete span. One could drive on the new road, or on the old road.

Of buildings, only the bridge's stone tollhouse, also built in 1820, could be seen from the dirt lane that led to the interior of the Youngs' property. A succession of tenants lived in it, even before 1924, when the state took over the road's maintenance and took away the tolls.

The Youngs continued to run the farm as a dairy operation. Dairying was the main legitimate occupation for lower Loudoun farmers from the 1920s through the '50s. But Mr. Young, as a lawyer, who also had an office in close-by Herndon, declined to sanction the bootlegging that was the main illegal occupation of lower Loudouners. Their brew was still concocted on the Potomac islands, and Selden's was often called Jenkins' Island during the early 20th century—the Jenkinses were still the prominent brewers. As had been the tradition, and since Miskel's had been owned by the Jenkinses during that era, they had moved their pints and quarts across the farmstead to the tollhouse.

The Youngs moved into one of the old Miskel places, not realizing it was the "historic one," the scene of the April 1, 1863, skirmish where Confederate partisan ranger John Singleton Mosby almost got his comeuppance. In honor of their farm's business, they would soon name the lane by the Miskels' house Dairy Lane.

After a year or so of dairy farming, Bob Young decided that getting up at 4 a.m. and being on call round the clock was not for him. So he decided to subdivide the farm, trusting it would reap greater rewards in fewer hours.

PHOTO COURTESY THOMAS BALCH LIBRARY, WINSLOW WILLIAMS COLLECTION

Broad Run Farms in 1952

He became a real estate agent. As a newcomer to the area, he needed an established partner and chose Coleman Gore, an affable Leesburg broker, to market the land. Mr. Gore emphasized the Indian connection rather than the Civil War one, and in his mailing to prospective buyers, he called the Potomac shore above Great Falls "as pure and beautiful as it was when the great Indian tribes inhabited the fabulous isle of Eden." Of course, the mailing noted the usual offerings of

> Rich Loudoun County, Virginia's most beautiful section. The lowest taxes, by far, in the metropolitan area…The best public schools in Virginia…free school bus…40 minutes to Washington…Gracious country living at its finest—[all] in the Heart of the Dogwood Country.

Messrs. Young and Gore mapped out a road network for the farm and added a 20-foot width of pavement to each travelway. At a spring by the farm's entrance and Route 7, Mr. Young had a lake dug out in 1952—an attractive come-on. The lake became a haven for fishing, bathing, and ice-skating, activities prohibited in this litigious society.

By the lake, Mr. Young had his tenants build him a small frame office, and on weekends he would wave down each car that passed. There weren't many. "He just waved us in," Muriel Spetzman told me. "My husband and I were driving down Route 7, and there he was by the road, arms flailing. He showed us a lot by Broad Run, and a whole bunch of ducks flew up from the water. We bought it practically instantly" in February 1952. One of Broad Run Farms' lanes was named Mallard Street.

Muriel and Lloyd Spetzman built their own home with redwood siding and pine interior. "We couldn't get to the land fast enough," Muriel said. "We'd come out every night from work in Washington." She said the house, with three bedrooms and two baths, cost about $4,000.

Other homes at the Farms were pricier. Mr. Young told me that the first house, built for U. S. Air Force Colonel William LaFayette Fagg, his wife Barbara, and their children, cost $30,000. The address of the brick Cape Cod-style home was 11 Broad Run Drive, and the Faggs' daughter lived there until spring of 2002. Bob Young's address was 7 Persimmon Lane; he gave Colonel Fagg the other lucky number because the two had been classmates at the University of Virginia law school. Colonel Fagg later became a brigadier general and was made provost marshal of the Air Force.

The second house in the Farms, a brick rambler with three bedrooms and one and a half baths, cost $21,069. That home was completed in October 1952, for Brit (pronounced *breet*) and the late Roy Peterson. Brit lives in it still and is the senior resident of the Farms. Showing me the exact cost breakdown, Brit Peterson pointed out that Roy had wired the novel General Electric remote-control lighting system. Roy, a researcher for the former Bureau of Ships in Washington, was not a licensed electrician, but the electrical inspector said Roy knew more about wiring than he did. Roy then wired nine other houses in the Farms. "The electricity inspection," Brit told me, "was the only permit we needed from the county."

The master builder for the Farms' first two houses was Bunt Smith, husband of Mildred Kidwell Smith, Sterling postmistress from 1939 to 1969. That he was a master was evident from the houses' prices, double that of the average area house during the early 1950s.

Brit had heard of the Farms when she spoke with Lucy, Coleman Gore's wife, at a Loudoun Women's Club picnic. When the Gores needed another real estate broker because they were thinking of marketing a smaller subdivision called Potomac Farms two miles west, Roy took up the weekend challenge. As Brit put it, "He became his own first customer" by buying the lot they would live on.

Lots in the Farms ranged from a half-acre to 10 acres bordering the Potomac's Little River. Most lots were one or two acres. Except for the 10-acre parcels, marketed at $10,000, all lots initially sold for $1,250. "First to come have first choice," newspaper ads said. The down payment was $100, with monthly payments of $25, including interest. The average local salary was then about $3,000 a year. By summer 1953, with more than 100 lots sold and 80 houses under construction, the price of the smaller lots rose to $2,000, with the same down payment and financing terms. A buyer also had to add another $2,000 or so to dig a well and install a septic field. The Farms had no public sewer system until 1995, when there were 230 houses in the community. Wells remain the only source for water.

One buyer of a 10-acre lot in the late 1950s was U. S. Senator Everett McKinley Dirksen (R-Ill.). While living at the Farms in 1959, he became minority leader of the U. S. Senate. At the Farms, Senator Dirksen is remembered for planting marigolds, even while he was living weekends in a trailer beside his future house, which he and wife, Louella, named "Heart's Desire." Senator Dirksen was so fond of the marigold that he wanted the District of Columbia to change its official flower from the American Beauty Rose to the marigold. Through the 1970s Broad Run Farms Civic Association bulletins pictured the flower and the words "Home of the Marigold."

Like Senator Dirksen, but without benefit of his chauffeured car, most breadwinners at the Farms commuted to Washington. The early-morning drive hardly was a rush hour until the first traffic light, across Chain Bridge at Arizona Avenue and Canal Road in Washington. The average driving time was 50 minutes—40 during usual hours.

Shaw Road, which jutted into the Leesburg Pike just opposite

Broad Run Drive, the Farms' main access road to the pike, became Sully Road in 1965. Robert Wagstaff, Fairfax County history buff, told B. Powell Harrison, one of the main backers of that road, "You've got to name it for Sully"—-Richard Bland Lee's 1794 Sully Plantation stood some 10 miles south of Route 7, and Mr. Wagstaff and others had persuaded Dulles Airport's planners not to demolish the house and outbuildings.

Powell Harrison, Realtor Herb Sumney, and several others wanted to improve and widen old Shaw Road, as there was then no access to Route 7 from Dulles Airport.So they went to see Congressman Howard W. Smith, stalwart area representative since 1931. Mr. Smith heard the group out, and replied with his characteristic "Don't worry boys, I'll take care of it." He did.

A prominent area house of newer vintage, once quite visible from the Farms' entrance, also still stands, by Broad Run at the southwest corner of the run and Route 7. Two interior decorators, Don McAfee of Washington and Tom Geiger of Loudoun, designed the French Provincial home. The home, completed in 1954, is often called the Quarry House, as it overlooks the water-filled quarry hole where stone was cut for the Broad Run bridge and tollhouse.

In 1965 Broad Run Farms' first public building, Galilee Methodist Church, arose by the lake. An integral part of the church's design was its wavy roofline with 14 crests. They symbolized the surface of Israel's fish-laden Sea of Galilee and were intended as a biblical reference to Matt. 4:19: "I will make you fishers of men." "The Lake," as Broad Run Farms residents generally called the body of water, officially became Lake Galilee.

Today, Broad Run Farms has 320 homes and 1,280 residents. Its longtime residents yet call it "The Farms," and it continues to develop in the casual manner that gives the community charm. An irregular street pattern, treed lots, and homes of all sizes, shapes, and textures—frame, brick, and concrete block—place the Farms in an eclectic category unique in the Virginia Piedmont.

Sterling Park
The First Big One

Before 1962 it was farmland crisscrossed by two unpaved roads south of the Leesburg Pike: the nearly parallel Vestal's Gap Road and from it veering southwest, the Church Road.

South of the pike and just west of the Fairfax County line was Jesse Hughes's dairy farm. Jesse was a newcomer. He'd come from Smythe County early in the century. He was a member of the board of supervisors in Smythe, and in Loudoun he became longtime head of the Democratic County Committee.

To the south there were smaller farms, and then one came to "Old Man" Walter Hummer's grass farm, its entry lane leading to the north side of Church Road. Walter was Loudoun from way back. He sold hay to the McLeans at Belmont.

South of Church Road the big spread belonged to the Edwards family. Samuel Edwin "Squire" Edwards (1861-1943) was the son of Charles Edwin Edwards and Alice Texas (Compton) Edwards. One story circulated that Samuel Edwin was an orphan, but that was only because his father, although born in Loudoun, married, resided, and died in Washington, D. C. Charles Edwin's father was Samuel Murray Edwards, who had served two separate terms as mayor of Leesburg.

In 1883, Samuel Edwin Edwards married Sarah Frances Keene, a daughter of Newton and Elizabeth (Dulin) Keene. The Keenes were the big area landowners of the 19th century. "Squire" Edwards was justice of the peace for years. His son, Lee E. Edwards, in 1930 built the barn that housed the first Sterling Park fire company and that now serves as a community center. Lee also drained the nearby farm pond; it used to be 12-feet deep in the center.

On the southwest fringes of future Sterling Park were vast stretches of Sterling Farm, owned by Fred Franklin Tavenner, "a little kin to Benjamin Franklin," he proudly told me in 1977. Fred had bought the land from Albert Shaw Jr., who had inherited it from his father, Albert B. Shaw (1857-1947), remembered about Sterling for both his literary and farming prowess.

The senior Shaw, who bided his time between Sterling Farm and an estate at Hastings-on-Hudson, New York, edited and published the American *Review of Reviews*, one of the first U. S. periodicals to feature discussions of current events. In 1912 he directed publication of the 10-volume *The Photographic History of the Civil War*, still the classic work of its genre.

Albert Shaw's spreads about Sterling totaled 1,640 acres. One tract was called "The Experimental Farm," for he was the first area farmer to receive a U. S. government grant for applying "scientific methods," as Mr. Tavenner recalled them, to the raising of crops and livestock. White Russians—1920s refugees from the Soviet Union—ran the farm for Mr. Shaw.

He would also drop in on the nearby Coleman's, Daysville, and Sterling schools, for he was interested in improving rural education for Southern youngsters—white youngsters only. Mr. Shaw was a staunch white supremacist. He not only supported Jim Crow laws, but sought to take the vote away from blacks who didn't meet his standards of enlightenment. He was a long-time member of both the Southern Education Board and General Education Board.

Fred Tavenner also bought the Robey Farm. Dr. William Isaiah Robey was a Herndon physician; his brother Ernest was town pharmacist. Dr. William had practiced in Herndon and in the Sterling area since the early 1900s, and after a stay in Alexandria and the District, came back to Herndon in the 1930s. He was a big man and had diabetes. He was a great man for ice cream, something he wasn't supposed to eat. But he'd always stop at Page's old store at Sterling and ask for a double dip. George Page knew the doctor was a diabetic and was worried about his ice cream intake. After some years George tried to broach the problem: "Dr. Robey, why does a doctor go to another doctor when sick?"

"My boy," said Dr. Robey, "on the theory that a sick man doesn't know what's good for him. Give me another dip of ice cream."

Delivering mail on old Sterling Route 1, from the Hugheses down to the Robeys, was Morris Hummer, "Old Man" Walter Hummer's brother. Morris carried the mail sacks on horseback and then in his Model T. By 1940, his son, Aubrey Lee Hummer, was carrying on the family tradition.

This was Sterling Park in the years before 1962.

It was probably in the late 1720s when tenants and slaves for the McCarty, Lee, and Carter families began to farm the region, and in 1777 an Englishman, Nicholas Cresswell, took stock of their farming procedures. "Their method is to clear a piece of land from the woods, generally put it in wheat the first year, Indian corn the next, and so alternately for six or seven years together. By that time the strength of the land is gone and they say it is worn out, throw it out to the woods again, and set about clearing another piece." This method of crop rotation became known as the "old field-new field" system of farming and until the Civil War it was commonplace throughout the South. The system was highly inefficient, for as the observant Mr. Cresswell noted, only half your arable land was being cultivated at one time.

And to boot, Sterling-area soils were clayey and not the best for farming. But then, Dr. Shaw was advised to invest in them at $13 an acre in 1908—a few dollars an acre more than average.

Fifty years later, area farmers were anticipating prices of $500 an acre. Rumblings were in the air about a new international airport near the Fairfax-Loudoun line. The area east of the village of Sterling and north of the old village of Willard (soon to be razed for the airport) was left unzoned. And in addition to the rumored airport, through the area came the two main transportation routes into Loudoun, the Leesburg Pike and the Washington and Old Dominion Railroad. And poking at the Loudoun boundary from Fairfax were the caps of sewer lines, awaiting their westward extensions.

In New York City, Lehman Brothers, one of the world's largest banking firms, soon made plans to buy up vast tracts along Broad Run and from Sterling west to Ashburn. By October 1959, as work on the new international airport was progressing and with many developers and politicians pushing for sewer lines to serve the area, Lehman Brothers, operating through a subsidiary, the Northern Virginia Development Corporation, had bought 2,047 acres for $1,415,000, roughly $700 an acre.

Marvin T. Broyhill Sr., however, felt Lehman Brothers had miscalculated: the awaited sewer lines would not go that far west. In 1959 and 1960 he formulated plans to assemble a large contiguous parcel—the future Sterling Park—east of the Lehman Brothers holdings.

In Fred Tavenner's words, "These Broyhills jumped on that thing way early. They put out those real-estate people and had them working day and night to get that land...I don't know whether people really knew for sure [of the Broyhills' reasons for buying]. They didn't think it would come so fast. They came to me before they came to anyone else. They offered me $1 million before they ever got even started."

Fred sold most of his farm to the Broyhills, but withheld some of his tracts along future Route 28, and of that road he recalled, "They [the Broyhills] found out where the road was planning to be built. They thought they could use that road for the main road through Sterling Park. Then they wouldn't have to build a [through] road. Powell Harrison [a backer of Route 28] got riled up about it." Route 28 was to be the gateway to the new airport. The new through road would be the present Sterling Boulevard.

"I gave them [the state] all that right-of-way for Route 28 for nothing"—about 11 acres. Mr. Tavenner's largesse would soon pay dividends, for as commercial interests noted the deed transfers they rushed to buy prime sites along future Route 28. Fred Tavenner sold 20 acres to Hot Shoppes for $100,000. "I didn't want to sell any of it," he told me, "but Mr. Hall [Leesburg's Wilbur Hall] talked me into it. He had always been my father's lawyer, and I had a lot of confidence in him." Hot Shoppes never built on the tract. "Then Holiday Inn came along," Fred continued. "They found out about Hot Shoppes coming in— $10,00 an acre I said, and they [Holiday Inn] accepted it. They paid me for 20 acres." The inn stands today.

The senior Mr. Broyhill was a Carolinian, smart as a whip and with an eye for good investment. He had been in business since 1908 and recently developed and built subdivisions in Hopewell and in McLean.

Land in eastern Loudoun, though officially called an agricultural zone, had just been zoned one house for each acre. Mr. Broyhill knew that legally Loudoun County had two options. To permit development with a septic tank on each acre, or to change the zoning to a category known as "planned community"—meaning smaller lots with a large tract of open space for recreational areas. The smaller lots would have to be served by a sewer system, but with a major airport soon to open, sewers were a foregone conclusion—only the date was uncertain.

In late winter 1961, Marvin T. Broyhill Sr. made his decision and on March 10 incorporated the Broyhill Land Corporation. His son

Marvin T. Broyhill Jr. became president, and a cousin, Thomas J. Broyhill, was vice-president.

Within the span of eight months, between April 28 and December 29, 1961, the Broyhill Land Corporation bought 1,762.157 contiguous acres for $2,115,783.76. There were 14 separate parcels; at least four had been bought by speculators prior to the Broyhill's buying spree. Nevertheless, the Broyhills obtained most of the land for about $1,000 an acre; for the 226-acre Hughes Farm along Route 7 they paid a premium $1,700 an acre.

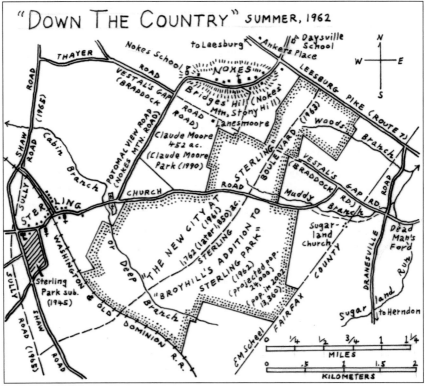

Marvin T. Broyhill Sr.'s idea was to put together a prefabricated home marketed by U. S. Steel and sell it for about $7,000, or $3,000 less than a comparable home in Fairfax County. In addition, the homes were to have central air-conditioning, unheard of in a home in that price range; and home owners were to have access—without membership fees—to golf and tennis courts and pools. An added selling point: Loudoun's taxes were less than half the taxes in Fairfax. Gas was cheap, and there was the possibility of opening up the Washington and Old Dominion Railroad to commuter traffic. Passenger service on the railroad had stopped in 1951. Except for golf and the railroad, abandoned by a 2-1 state Commerce Commission vote in 1971, all of the senior Mr. Broyhill's ideas are realities today.

"The Proposed New City at Sterling," as the *Loudoun Times-Mirror* called the project, was unveiled to the county on that newspaper's pages, August 17, 1961. One of the Broyhills (the paper did not state who) told editor Fitzhugh Turner that the development would be the finest planned community in America, and economist James C. Bishop presented figures stating that if you didn't take into account capital investment, the development would return more money to the county than the cost of schooling children and providing police and other services. Throughout the ensuing controversy of more than a year, no county government official, employed or elected, was able to come up with a mathematical alternative to Mr. Bishop's figures.

Four days later the map of the development was presented to the Loudoun Board of Supervisors. Board minutes indicate there was no comment, but ThomasJ. Broyhill did invite the board to travel at "Broyhills' expense to Louisville, Kentucky, and New Albany, Indiana, to inspect plants where the fabricated homes were to be made." The board declined with four abstentions; Joshua Fletcher, of Mercer district and Dr. William P. Frazer, of Jefferson district, voted no. While those were the days of steak-dinner diplomacy, the introduction before the board was not an auspicious one.

On February 22, 1962, the county board of supervisors, the county planners, and the Broyhills' men—James Bishop, attorney Thomas Mays, and engineer Sidney O. Dewberry—confronted one another in a six-hour hearing. *Times-Mirror* editor Fitzhugh Turner remarked that "four hours were given to the experts, none of whom vote in Loudoun County, and two hours were given to the amateurs, all of whom can vote in Loudoun County."

Maybe before that epic hearing, maybe after, county planner Doug Pratt, with the agreement of the planning commission, recommended the area of the Broyhill development be rezoned to a planned-community district (all county planning-commission minutes before 1965 have been lost or misplaced; "records had a habit of walking away," notes a former county official).

Broyhills' men said their planned community was to house 8,600 families: 6,600 in homes, 2,000 in apartments. They had already invested $2.5 million in the project, and if the board of supervisors didn't approve the recommended planned-community zoning, development would immediately begin; 547 acres into 1,700 house lots. The interest crunch had begun to show.

John Wallace of Red Hill, near Aldie, said the planned community would make Loudoun "the garden-spot of the U. S. A." Edward Stettinius of Middleburg asked where the money would come from to educate the youngsters. Erskine Bedford of Upperville suggested the county develop two rates of taxation. Jennings Potts of Hillsboro said farmers needed tax relief, not increased taxes because of new schools. Most onlookers at the hearing were not against the planned community; they were against growth.

Of importance to the project's eventual approval, the Broyhills had offered to pay an unprecedented $250 a household to the Loudoun County School Board. The Broyhills said the offer would stand even if they didn't receive planned-community zoning. An unnamed board member had warned that it was a donation for selfish reasons. J. Terry Hirst of Purcellville, Mt. Gilead district supervisor, and Joshua Fletcher felt the figure should be $300 a household, the figure they believed it cost to educate a child in 1962. [In 2002 that figure stands at $7,699.] The board voted 4-2 to postpone a decision.

Faced with the warning that the Broyhills might try to develop their lots using septic tanks, one on each acre, the board agreed to the rezoning for a planned community on May 7, 1962. Mr. Fletcher and J. Terry Hirst voted against the new zone. But two weeks later, because someone forgot to place public notices in the Sterling area, notifying people of the rezoning proposal, the board rescinded its motion.

Meanwhile, the plat for section one of "Broyhill's Addition to Sterling Park" had been filed with the clerk's office and had been dedicated on May 15, 1962. The plat, clearly the same as today's section one of Sterling Park, was masterminded by Sidney O. Dewberry and was remarkably similar to the plat printed by the *Loudoun Times-Mirror* a half-year before. As recommended by the planning staff, the lots had been increased from 9,000 square feet with 70 feet of frontage to 11,000 square feet with a typical lot measuring 75 by 102 feet.

One of the Broyhills, probably Marvin T. Sr., had thought of the name Sterling Park. But because of the 1945 Sterling Park subdivision southwest of Sterling village, the Broyhills' project had to have another name. Loudoun County did not allow two subdivisions to have the same name. So, "Broyhill's Addition to Sterling Park" became and still is the official name, even though the two subdivisions are not connected.

The original Sterling Park and "Broyhill's Addition" had one concenpt in common. Residents had to be of the "Caucasian Race." No board member or speaker before the board verbally objected to the clause, a common one in the U. S. through the 1960s, even though discriminatory housing had been outlawed by the Civil Rights Act of 1866. Not until August, 1966, when"The Park"—by then the subdivision's nickname—had 5,000 residents, did the first black family move in.

On June 21, 1962, the board once more approved planned-community zoning by a vote of 3-2. J. Terry Hirst and Joshua Fletcher were against, with board member Silas D. Phillips of Leesburg District and Dr. William P. Frazer voting yes, somewhat in a spirit of resignation. J. Emory Kirkpatrick, supervisor of Broad Run district, in whose district the new development would be voted a more enthusiastic "Yes." Erskine Bedford, an Upperville area farmer, said the action "could break the back of every farmer in Loudoun County in a few years."

Looking back at the situation with 20 years' hindsight, Silas Phillips said, "I didn't think anybody [in Leesburg District] wanted it, but there was nothing we could do about it." Dr. William Frazer believed it was better to have controlled growth in the eastern part of the county and then attempt to keep the county's western land for farming and rural purposes.

While the June 21 vote was the crucial one, Loudoun's planning commission still had to rezone the area from one house an acre to a planned community zone. The Broyhills' lawyer, Thomas G. Mays, and their economist, James Bishop, now became the lead spokesmen for Sterling Park. Following is a typical interchange between the pair and the planning commission, in the person of Tom Delashmutt, himself a developer.

Lest Mr. Bishop's figures be disputed by the commission, he was introduced as a graduate of Harvard Business School. Bishop was right on the button in regard to his projected .86 children per added home, but he also said that by 1968 the Broyhills' Addition to Sterling Park would realize a net profit to the county of $278,200 a year.

Delashmutt: "But Mr. Bishop you neglected to include capital improvements, mainly the new schools, and the cost of interest to the county. The development, in reality, is going to cost the county money."

Lawyer Mays, noting that economist Bishop is having trouble answering, takes over, but concedes in a small voice: "No doubt about that."

Delashmutt: "We are going to be out of pocket money in the end."

Mays: "Some money for capital expense."

The exchange was symbolic of numerous others. Any negative impact of the development had to be "squeezed out" of Sterling Park's staffers. And when confronted with that mode of operation they countered, "Oh, we were about to get to that point."

PHOTO COURTESY THOMAS BALCH LIBRARY

Patterns of the future, Sterling Park, 1983

Sometime in September or October of 1962 both the planning staff and commission recommended a vote for the planned community, with these major stipulations: increase lot sizes from 9,000 to 11,000 square feet, increase school sites from 12 to 14 acres, reduce apartment areas from 256 to 140 acres, and reduce commercial areas from 125 to 65 acres. The Broyhills agreed, and on October 22, 1962, by unanimous vote of the board of supervisors, Sterling Park became a reality.

After the vote, Erskine Bedford, representing western Loudoun conservation groups, warned that "an excess of $100 will have to come from every man, woman and child in Loudoun for costs of capital outlay for schools." A week before, county farmers had asked the board to assess their land for its use value, not its real-estate value. That saving grace would come to pass in 1972..

On February 14, 1963 Tom Terry and Janet L. Brooks and Paul T. and Dorothy T. Stone bought the first properties in Broyhills' Addition to Sterling Park. A day later there were six other buyers: Donald Arthur and Betty Lee McGill, Joseph T. and Victoria J. Gooding, Kenneth Eric and Mary A. Carlson, Harry Donald and Lucinda D. Fitzner, Emmanuel and Christine A. Lopez, and Alfred H. and Doris Ann LaPlaca. Puchase prices ranged between $14,800 and $21,900. Four of these couples still lived in Sterling Park in 1981, when their investments had tripled.

Broyhills' team named the homes for Loudoun County communities with one exception: the "Glen Ora" was named for President John F. Kennedy's weekend retreat south of Middlburg in Fauquier County. The top-of-the-line model at $21,900 was the "Arcola," while the "Hillsboro" and "Wheatland" were the least expensive models in the $14–15,000 range. In between were the "Ashburn," "Bluemont," "Hamilton," "Leesburg," "Middleburg," "Waterford," and "Glen Ora."

The price ranges were well within the development's modest initial covenants: No dwelling was to cost less than $10,000; the minimum square footage of a one-story house was to be 890; of a two-story house, 1,390. No house could exceed two and one-half stories or have a garage that could hold more than two cars.

Planning commissioner George Horkan, the Upperville attorney, was worried that the "low-cost" homes would evolve into a slum area, and judging from other comments and letters to the *Loudoun Times-Mirror*, this fear of "crackerboxes" was an overriding one for those desiring to uphold Loudoun's position as the wealthiest rural county in Virginia.

Nineteen years after the controversy I spoke with Sidney O. Dewberry, engineer of the Sterling Park development plan. He first recalled that Marvin T. Broyhill Sr.'s input into the plan was less than might have been expected from the head of a development that size. He then said that Mr. Broyhill wanted to attract couples in their late twenties with one or two children. They needed a house from $5,000 to $10,000 less than a comparable house in Fairfax County. They did not "need an upscale" Reston, then in its planning stages. In all probability, Marvin T. Broyhill felt that such amenities as greenbelts and common space would not be as marketable as a house on a quarter-acre lot.

Now, forty years after the controversy, Sterling Park has changed its demograpahics from 1966, when the first African American family moved in among 1,500 white households. The county's population expert, Clark Draper, told me in June, 2002, that of The Park's 13,360 persons, 9,806 or 73 percent are white, 1,153 are Asian, and 1,049 are black. There are 1,785 Hispanics included in the above three categories.

PHOTO COURTESY THOMAS BALCH LIBRARY

Indeed, the first Big One, in 1970

Sugarland Run

The name was coined in 1692, at the very latest, for when David Strahan and his "Rangers of Pottomack" visited the area that September 22 he casually mentioned "we came to a great Runn that made into the suggar land." Next day he noted in his journal, "We marcht to the suggar land and, the 24th we ranged about to see if we could find the trace of any Indians but we not see any fresh sign."

Lieutenant Strahan, when he was not leading scouting parties, was operating the first ferry across the Occoquan River, and his rangers were commissioned by Governor Sir Francis Nicholson to monitor Indian activity. Two months earlier the governor had come to the area and reported that "upper parts of the Potomac were much affrighted by mischief done near the falls on both sides of the river."

Area Indians of the Algonkian-speaking tribes possibly gave the area its name. Historian Robert Beverley, writing about Strahan's expedition in 1705, noted the rangers had observed "an inspissate Juice, like Molasses, distilling from the Tree. The Heat of the Sun had candied some of this juice, which gave the Men a Curiosity to taste it. They found it sweet and by this Process of Nature learn'd to improve it into Sugar. But these Trees growing so far above the Christian Inhabitants, it hath not yet been tried whether Quantity or Quality it may be worth while to cultivate this Discovery...yet it has been known among the Indians longer than any now remember."

David Strahan and his men were the first known party to enter present-day Loudoun. Seven years later, in 1699, the third known team of explorers, Burr Harrison and Giles Vandercastle, "lay at the sugarland" on April 16. Another early entry of the name appears August 10, 1757, the first tavern to receive its license in the new county of Loudoun was James Coleman's "at the Sugar-lands."

These original sugar-lands, though, encompassed a far greater expanse than today's 541-acre Sugarland Run community. The Sugarlands, named for sugar maples extended for a mile or so on each side of Sugarland Run from the Potomac south to Herndon. Coleman's lay near the southern boundary, at Dead Man's Hollow by the ford where the old Church Road crosses Sugarland Run. Back in the 18th century the road in this section (then the main road from Alexandria to Winchester) was often called the Sugarland Path.

The present Sugarland Run community was part of the first grant of land in Loudoun to Captain Daniel McCarty of Westmoreland County, 2,993 acres "above the falls of the Potowmack River, beginning on said River side at the lower end of the Sugar Land Island opposite the upper part of the rocks in said River." Sugar Land Island was then called McCarty's Island for many years, and in the late 19th century the island began to be known by its present name, Lowe's Island, for owner John H. Lowe.

Captain McCarty received the grant on Feb. 2, 1709. He was a member of the Virginia General Assembly from 1705 until his death in 1724, and married Ann, the sister of Thomas Lee, subsequent owner, of most of the property west to Goose Creek. The McCartys of Westmoreland County owned most of the land, known as their Sugarland Quarter through the 18th century. Charles Eskridge, clerk of the Loudoun Court, owned much of the land in the early 19th century.

In 1857 some of the Sugarland Quarter passed to John Austin of Georgetown, Maryland (now D. C.). He paid $8,120 for 457 acres, most of today's Sugarland Run community. John Austin willed the land to his wife Jane Austin in 1868, and she gave the tract to her daughter Georgia Carper. Until the land was last farmed in 1967, it was known as the Carper Farm.

The road leading to the Carper Farm was known as Scott's Road or Scott's Landing Road through much of the 19th century. Mr. Scott took care of a warehouse that stored goods awaiting shipment across the Potomac River to the Chesapeake and Ohio Canal. During Civil War times the road was also known as Rowzer's Ford Road, for the Rowzie family—spellings were approximate in those times—living on the Maryland side of the Potomac ford—the deepest ford on the river.

Carper Farm passed out of the family in 1919 when John A. Carper sold its 457 acres to A. Page Wrenn for $14,000. Wrenn ran a general farming operation; livestock and crops, mainly corn, heat, oats, rye— the same crops that had been growing for more than a century. During the late 19th century and early 20th century the neighborhood was known as Daysville, for the nearby 1869-1907 post office by that name. Since the early 20th century the road has been called Potomac View Road, after Cecil Duff's Potomac View Farm, a 1,600-acre tract to the north and west of Carper Farm.

Six days after "Black Tuesday," October 29, 1929, the day the stock market fell, Page Wrenn took a loss on Carper Farm and sold the 457 acres for $13,250. One of the Depression era owners of the Carper place was an Oklahoman who had a taste for showgirls and airplanes. He is said to have brought the first plane into Loudoun—aside from the many that barnstormed at Wallace George's cowpasture in Leesburg after World War I. The Okie finally crashed the plane—he'd land it anywhere—but walked out unscathed. After George Page's Sterling Mercantile got its beer license back after enactment of the 19th Amendment repealing Prohibition, the Okie would always make a big show in the store by illegally (in Virginia) opening up the bottles and "treating the boys."

Colonel John F. Hepner brought stability back to Carper in 1937, when he bought the farm back from the bank for $7,500. Colonel Hepner was a cavalry man in charge of the remount station at Front Royal. His brother Oliver Hepner farmed the tract and converted the buildings into a dairy operation. During the late 1940s, 72 Holsteins and Guernseys roamed Carper. Burl Bowles, Colonel Hepner's last farm manager, shipped out the last stock cows late in 1967. In 30 years the Hepners realized a profit of more than a million dollars; their selling price to Louis Zuckerman and Gerald Luria, the owners of Shadyside, a Maryland development company, was $1,308,000.

Shadyside sold out on April 28, 1969, to Boise Cascade Building Corporation, a division of Boise Cascade, a growing concern, yet to break the nation's top 225, specializing in paper products. Shadyside sold the land, now 541 acres, to Boise for $1,840,800.

Sugarland Run was the logical name, the choice of Boise Cascade when it planned its development, slated for two and one-half dwellings to the acre. However, Beckham W. Dickerson Jr., Loudoun's planning director, felt, correctly, that the county did not want to see 541 acres of homes, each sitting on a 17,500-square-foot plot. Mr. Dickerson proposed to the Loudoun County Planning Commission that the county develop a "planned community" zone that would cluster some dwellings, and therefore leave about 20 percent of the land in open space. In addition, to encourage variety, restrictions regarding such items as the set-back of homes from the road were to be flexible.

Mr. Dickerson drew up plans for the new zone, and at the same time encouraged Boise Cascade to plan its community within the zone's guidelines. It did, and the plan of Earl Ottinger and others of the California firm of Stottler, Stagg & Associates passed the planning commission, and then the Loudoun County Board of Supervisors on August 1969. There was the barest rustle of opposition.

Not one person spoke against Sugarland Run, and only one, Vinton Liddell Pickens of Janelia Farm up the pike questioned that 400 acres was too small a tract for a planned community. After the board rather matter-of-factly approved Beckham Dickerson's new ordinance and his concept for Sugarland Run, it got down to the business of discussing Marcus Bles's proposed exposition of science and industry on his land to the west of Broad Run Farms. Again, speaking up against a host of realtors and businessmen, was Vinton Pickens—the initial force behind the county's first zoning ordinance of 1942. She felt the Route 7 corridor should remain open.

Perhaps murmurs against Sugarland Run were few because only a week before the planning commission approved the Sugarland Run plan, it had defeated a Levitt and Sons development, 1,270 acres and a projected 15,000 people, just to the west. The late Les King, then director of Loudoun's Soil Conservation Service, deserves credit for squelching Levitt. He knew that about a half-mile east of Goose Creek there stood an old walnut tree on the the Potomac bottom. On the tree were notched marks noting the high-water levels of the 1889 and 1936 floods. Les figured that the marks, respectively, were at 214.43 and 208.43 inches, and with these measurements proved Levitt incorrect in their determination of the 100-year flood plain.

Looking back at Sugarland Run some 30 years later, Beck Dickerson feels the county can be proud it had the courage to pursue a new concept rather than fall back on an old course. And it was the old course that hit Loudoun pocketbooks that summer of 1969. Reassessments doubled from the previous year and Broad Run District, home of Sterling Park with 8,300 people, experienced an average rise of 40 percent.

Sugarland Run's first homes were ready for occupancy by January

1971, and on the 20th of that month Sheila and Leslie Clarke, their three children, Darin, Lynette, and Derek, their black Labrador, Blackie and silver poodle, Fresca, became the first residents at 30 Thrush Road. A few days later they were joined by Nancy and Gary Howell and daughters Linda and Nancy.

By the end of May, 41 families had bought homes costing between $28,000 and $35,000, the same price range of single-family homes in nearby Sterling Park. By the close of 1971 almost 225 homes were sold, and in 1972 there were about 540 sales. Buyers were attracted by open-interiors—high ceilings—and a spacious Mediterranean look. Model homes sported Spanish and Mexican furniture and sundries a la Dockside, a popular and stylish home-furnishing store of the time.

Sugarland buyers were in their upper 20s or low 30s, had two children under 10, and had a few pets. Most of the buyers were from the Washington metropolitan area, and several had moved from Reston and Sterling Park. More Sugarland buyers worked for the federal government than did Sterling Park buyers, and thus the average Sugarland income was a bit higher than that of Sterling Park.

Some shoddy construction and grading overshadowed the stylish look of homes by late 1971. And through the next year a rash of complaints hit the Loudoun Board of Supervisors: joints were coming apart, and basements were leaking and flooding due to faulty earth moving. Flooding was widespread when Tropical Storm Agnes moved through Loudoun in June of 1972. In February 1972 the board refused to approve the 250-unit townhouse section until the complaints were rectified. Boise Cascade lumber was okay, but the firm did not have the building and development experience to use its products to the best advantage.

Back in 1969, Frederick A. Kober, Boise's head man in Loudoun, had told the board supervisors: "We do not plan to develop one piece of property and leave. We are here to stay." Famous last words: Spring of '72 saw Kober back in Boise, Idaho. In April 1972, Boise Cascade sold the unbought sections of Sugarland Run to Larwin Atlantic, a subsidiary of CNA Financial Corporation. Construction complaints continued. People wouldn't pay. Larwin and Larwin sued hundreds. Things weren't straightened out until a few years later.

Sugarland Run had been billed as Loudoun's second planned community—Sterling Park being the first. Neither community fulfilled or fulfills today the true meaning of the phrase "planned community," mainly because most residents have to drive elsewhere to work. And while Sterling Park has some industry, it does not have the amenities and open space Sugarland Run has. Sterling does not have a homeowners' association, while by 1971, Sugarland Run had two, one for townhouses, the other for detached homes.

These associations, the norm for planned communities, were the first in Loudoun County, and provided services and maintenance and told the homeowner what he could or couldn't do to his property.

But at Sugarland Run most breadwinners were more concerned about the commute to Washington, in the early seventies pushing an hour. It's closer today to two. But now more of the Run's nearly 2,000 workers have jobs in the Virignia suburbs. The remaining 3,225 stay at home or go to school. Unless birthrates increase dramatically, the community never will reach its initial projections of 7,600 persons—small consolation to drivers.

Placing Sugarland Run in perspective with other eastern Loudoun developments, the county's population expert, Clark Draper, tells me next-door CountrySide has 7,200 folk, Ashburn Farm tops 10,900, and Ashburn Village bests 11,800. Broadlands and South Riding are coming up on the outside.

Acknowledgment

Our thanks to the following persons for their time, effort and for their special memories. Without their generosity, the preservation of these recollections would not have been possible.

Mary Fleming Ankers, George Atwell, Aline Bailey, Betty Banks, Joseph E. Beard, L. Hunter Blevins, Randy Breton, Benjamin Bridges, Gertrude Bridges, Nellie Burton, Rosie M. Bushrod, Ed Byrne, Mr. and Mrs. Fred H. Byrne, Robert F. Byrne, Mary A. Carlson, Eileen Carlton, J. C. Church, Emma Clark, Sheila, Leslie, and Derek Clarke, Pat Clear, Elizabeth LeFevre Cooke, John C. Costello, Anna S. Day, Sidney O. Dewberry, Beckham W. Dickerson Jr., Rick Donaldson, Ned Douglass, Richard Dove, May Maddox Dowden, Clark Draper, James R. Eberly, Mrs. Frank E. Farrar, Dr. William P. Frazer, Gordon Fletcher, Gordon P. Fletcher Jr., Thomas Brook Grimes, Coleman C. Gore, Gerry Gardner, Joseph T. Gooding, the Rev. Homer A. Hall, Diane Hammond, John C. Hawkins, Anna Hedrick, Arlean Hill, J. Terry Hirst, Margaret Lail Hopkins, Daisy Hutchison, John Hutchison, Louisa S. Hutchison, Thomas B. Hutchison, Asa Moore Janney, Rebecca LeVan Stevenson Jackson, Albert Jenkins, J. Emory Kirkpatrick, Doris Ann LaPlaca, David LeRoy, John G. Lewis, Bernie Sullivan Light, Herbert D. Maddox, Mr. and Mrs. E. Ferne Marshall, Louise Sowers Marshall, Jean McDonald, Marie Tyler McGraw, Carl McIntyre, the Reverend Glen D. McLaughlin, Sadie Middleton, Claude H. Mitchell, Charles S. Monroe, Dr. Claude Moore, Aline Bailey Newman, Mary E. Newman, Carrie and Clarence Nokes, Jane Norman, George H. Page, Harry L. Pangle, Virginia Peacock, Tessie Penn, Brit Peterson, John T. Phillips II, Margaret Phillips, Silas D. Phillips, Mr. and Mrs. C. Preston Poland, Charles P. Poland Jr., Alda Watson Popovich, Winston Porter, Roger F. Powell,

Douglas M. Pratt, Tom Quinn, Sally Reed Rich, Robert M. Richardson, Charles Franklin Riticor, Charles Roberts, Nancy G. Rogers, Nellie Glascock Rutherford, Charles Sager, Harry A. Sager Jr., Mazie Sue Schulz, Mary Virginia Shockley, Rachel Shockley, Kitty Slater, Eugenia B. Smith, the Reverend Harold Smith, Mildred Smith, C. Lester Solomon, Malachi G. Spence, Muriel Spetzman, Frank L. Spitzer, Dorothy T. Stone, John Stone, Herbert Sumney, Mary Sullivan, Jane Chinn Sween, Gordon and Mary Gail Swenson, C. Blair Tavenner, Fred Franklin Tavenner, Eleanor Lee Templeman, Margaret W. Testerman, Fitzhugh Thomas, Golden Thornton, Jeanette Scott Thornton, Munday Tillett, Bill Tillett, Joe Trocino, Helen Wallace, and Robert B. Young.

Bibliography

No book has covered the history of lower Loudoun. One book, Louis Hutchison's *Come America To a Land of Simple Pleasures,* published in 1983 at the author's expense, contains 10 pages of recollections of Carter's School in the 1920s.

For other published reminiscences we turn to newspapers, notably J. Harry Shannon's "Rambler" columns in the *Washington Star,* 1912 - 1927, and my 1976-to-present columns in the *Loudoun Times-Mirror, Leesburg Today,* and *The Washington Post.* Many snippets from these detailed articles, especially from the *Times-Mirror* appear in this volume and will grace subsequent volumes of the *Loudoun Discovered* series.

One might also peruse these following newspaper essays about four notable residents: Francis Lightfoot Lee, Margaret Mercer, John W. Jones, and Roger F. Powell. All appeared under my byline in the "Loudoun Extra" sections of *The Washington Post:* Lee, April 21, 2002; Mercer, March 17, 2002; Jones, July 7, 2002; and Powell, September 2, 2001.

For more extensive reading about Lee, see *Francis Lightfoot Lee: The Incomparable Signer,* by Alonzo Thomas Dill, published by the Virginia Independence Bicentennial Commission, Williamsburg, circa 1976.

Added information on Miss Mercer appears in Byron A. Lee's *The Mercers and Parkhurst,* published by the author in 1999, at Harwood, Maryland.

A Mercer academy alumnus, John Morris Wampler, receives accolades in *Confederate Engineer* by George G. Kundahl, University of Tennessee Press, Knoxville, 2000.

Turning to overall county histories, the best and only one worth its salt is Charles Preston Poland Jr.'s *From Frontier to Suburbia,* published in 1979 at Marceline, Missouri, by Walsworth Publishing.

Full of exquisite detail, though only for the county's first decade, is John Phillips II's *The Historian's Guide to Loudoun County,* volume 1, issued by Phillips's Goose Creek Productions in 1996.

Details of another memorable era in the county's history, the Great Depression, are covered in my *Loudoun Times-Mirror* series, Feb. 18, 25; Mar. 4, 11, 18, 1982

For a short read, try my chronological "1,000 Years of Loudoun," issued by *The Washington Post* in 2000. This compendium initially ap-

Fairfax Harrison's 1924 classic, *Landmarks of Old Prince William,* reprinted at least twice, covers a myriad of subjects from the American Indian era of the 17th century through to the early 1800s. Mr. Harrison's aristocratic prose may delight, but the book's organization can baffle. Footnotes are lengthy and erudite.

The Guide to Loudoun, my 1975 "little Baedecker," has three driving and two walking tours of eastern Loudoun, at the time mostly rural.

In reference to the W. & O. D. Railroad, lifeline of lower Loudoun for a century, see Herbert H. Harwood Jr.'s *Rails to the Blue Ridge...1847-1968.* The Northern Virginia Park Authority published its third edition in 2000. In 1969 the Arlington Historical Society published a companion volume, *Washington & Old Dominion Railroad, 1847-1968,* by Ames W. Williams.

For the Loudoun Branch Railroad of the 1850s see my piece in the *Post's* "Loudoun Extra" edition, March 11, 2001. An accompanying map shows the railroad's entire right-of-way, also defined on my far larger 1990 map of Loudoun County.

That eastern Loudoun was once *Cameron Parish in Colonial Virginia—* is explored in the book written and privately printed by Margaret Lail Hopkins in 1988.

Eastern Loudoun from 1757-1798 is now western Fairfax. For background of the region west of Difficut Run and Little Rocky Run, see Beth Mitchell's *Beginning at a White Oak...,* published by Fairfax County in 1977, with a map showing land-grant boundaries at a scale of 1 inch equals 4,000 feet.

Charles P. Poland Jr.'s *Dunbarton, Dranesville, Virginia,* published by Fairfax County in 1974 explores the northerly section of this region in detail.

The southern section is covered well in Eugenia B. Smith's *Centreville: Its History and Architecture,* another Fairfax County publication, 1973.

A classic plantation biography is Robert S. Gamble's *Sully: The Biography of a House,* written in 1973 and published by The Sully Foundation, Chantilly.

That eastern Loudoun developed in a manner that raped the region of historic sites, leads me to mention the four-part history of planning

and zoning in the *Loudoun Times-Mirror*, October 9, 16, 23, 30, 1986. Brian Chitwood and I authored the articles.

Several maps of more-than-passing interest: First, the 1853 effort of Yardley Taylor, titled *Map of Loudoun County, Virginia, from Actual Surveys*. Published in color by Thomas Reynolds and Robert Pearsall Smith of Philadelphia, the map's scale is 1 mile equals one and three-eighths inches (approx). The Janney brothers, natives of Mr. Taylor's Lincoln, reprinted the map at a scale of 1 inch equals 1 mile. The U. S. Topographical Engineers' 1862 [Map of]*North-Eastern Virginia and Vicinity of Washington* draws heavily from Yardley Taylor's map.

Of recent vintage, my 1982 map, *One-Half Hour From Washington Dulles Airport*—the map that named the airport—shows, in addition to major historic and archeological sites, zoning, and water, sewer, and gas-transmission lines. The map's scale is 1 inch equals 1 mile.

My 1994 map, *The Tri-Counties of Upper Prince William–Lower Loudoun–East Fauquier*, scale 1 inch equals seven-eighths of a mile (approx.), covers the history of the area south of the old Loudoun Branch Railroad.

And concerning all of eastern Loudoun is Wynne C. Saffer's 2002 volume, unpublished but bound, titled "1850 Land Tax Maps, Thomas M. Wrenn's District." In it properties of 10 or more acres (their owners named) are platted on the most recent 1:24,000 Geological Survey maps.

The U. S. Post Office Department's circa 1915 *Rural Delivery Routes, Loudoun County, Virginia* is the next detailed map of the entire county to follow that of Mr. Taylor. Its scale,1 inch equals 1 mile. Piggybacking on that map, at the same scale, but in color, is Oscar L. Emerick's 1923 map showing public schools, simply titled *Loudoun County, Virginia*.

U. S. Coast and Geodetic Survey, Geological Survey, and Army Map Service 1:125,000, 1:62,500, and 1:24,000 maps of the 1880s through 1960s show the then-slow patterns of growth. As an adjunct, the 1937 and 1950 aerial photgraphs, 1 inch equals1,320 feet, flown by the U. S. Soil and Conservation Service, are valuable in regard to where structures once stood, and where old roads cut through the landscape. The clarity of the 1937 photos remains unexcelled.

Virginia's highway department, now VDOT, has issued county road maps since 1932, with that year's map names the roads as well as giving numbers that were changed in 1936. Editions of the 1940s and '50s also show rural and village buildings, often in a less-than-accurate manner. The maps' scale: 1 inch equals 2 miles.

The American Indian presence, dating from about 10,000 B. C. and lasting until the early 18th century is covered in general terms by William F. Rust III in *Loudoun County Prehistory,* published by his now-defunct Loudoun Archaeology Center in 1986.

An overview of findings from area prehistoric occupations, *The Prehistoric People of Accokeek Creek,* by Robert L. Stephenson, was published at Accokeek, Maryland, by the Alice Ferguson Foundation in 1959.

A typical eastern Loudoun archaeological study is the Iroquois Research Institute's *The Cultural Resources of Lowes Island, Virginia,* funded by the Fairfax County Water Authority in 1978. If this study is valuable in any way, it is for the detailed section on Jeb Stuart's crossing of the Potomac on his way to Gettysburg, June 27, 1863. Major General Stuart crossed at Rowzie's (Rowser's) Ford from Lowe's Island.

Another island, Selden's, is the focus of prehistoric excavations by Richard G. Slattery. See his scholarly "A Prehistoric Indian site on Selden Island, Montgomery County, Md.," in *Journal of the Washington Academy of Sciences,* 36, 8 (April 15, 1946).

Index

A complete index of the people, organizations, buildings, roads, events, and other matters included in *Loudoun Discovered* would contain well over 10,000 entries. To facilitate searching for this information, two approaches have been taken.

First, each volume includes a summary index, such as that which follows, of the information which features most prominently in the volume.

Second, a full text search capability covering all five volumes of *Loudoun Discovered* can be accessed through the website of the Friends of the Thomas Balch Library. See www.balchfriends.org.